WINE FOR TODAY

WINE FOR TODAY

JOHNNIE CRADOCK

With an introduction by
FANNY CRADOCK

FREDERICK MULLER LIMITED

First published in Great Britain 1975
by Frederick Muller Limited, London NW2 6LE

Copyright © John Whitby Cradock

ISBN 0 584 10344 1

Printed in Great Britain by The Anchor Press Ltd
and bound by Wm Brendon & Son Ltd
both of Tiptree, Essex

To Jill

Without whose constant help and encouragement this book
would never have seen the light of day.

Contents

Illustrations

INTRODUCTION

It is extremely difficult for any one as close as I am to Johnnie to write a completely unbiased introduction to this book.

He and I have always worked together in the closest possible ways, from cooking together on stage and television to travelling together all over the world. There are, however, certain areas in which our work has quite naturally slipped into specific divisions. For example, when it comes to travel, he does all the planning; he arranges all our schedules, and when on the ground he takes all our pictures. In fact for a great number of years he went around the world slung with cameras like a carpet seller from Baghdad and only the very recent cutting down of space in our newspapers has truncated this lucrative side of our travel writing. If we are making films, then he is the camera man, while I double up as performer and continuity girl – excellent training, for developing the powers of observation! Thus it has become automatic for me to spot the most modest brand name and the most minute trade label, by which we might otherwise fall into the unforgivable trap of 'plugging-by-visual' any implement or ingredient on a TV cookery show.

On the larger issue of our cookery work it has always been he who has won more wine decorations than I. Conversely, it has always been I who have won more cookery decorations than he. Thus I have always deferred to him over wine, and he gives me the last word on food. When we are entertaining, I plan the menus and hand them to him. He makes the vital wine-marriages for me and I have learned over the years to have a very healthy respect for his nose, palate and general vinous judgement.

Since we have both chosen to return to our first loves – writing – and have enough commissioned books to keep us out of mischief for a great many years, we have had occasion to look back over our long and infinitely rewarding, shared career. On one such recent raking over of the coals we discovered, to my immense pleasure anyway, that one little book of Johnnie's has sold more consistently than any similar book of mine.

This very small book, published originally at the huge price of five shillings, was and is called *The A.B.C. of Wine*. It is still selling, is in its umpteenth edition – we have both lost count – and looks as if it is going to rival Miss Agatha Christie's play, *The Mousetrap*, for longevity.

Then one day this huge, shattering new vinous situation developed with shocking celerity. The first I knew of it was when Johnnie announced that he had bought rather a lot of Champagne, a wine to which I am particularly partial at 11 a.m., more especially when accompanied by a dozen oysters! I remember Johnnie saying 'It will become rarer than gold dust and quite hideously expensive.' The rest of the sad tale you will all know by now. The excessive purchasing by the U.S.A.; the increased vinous consumption throughout Europe; the developing trend, for great table wines, with great long-keeping potentials to be drunk far too young; the resultant shortages and the colossal escalation in prices which eventually caused a complete revolution in the wine trade and drove shoppers into hitherto unexplored, practically unconsidered wine-growing areas which had previously been regarded as unworthy of their attentions.

This is what this book is about. It accepts the situation. It establishes the comforting fact that there are agreeable, honest, palatable table wines which can still be bought, despite current mountain-goat leapings into ruinous price-brackets, by those of us who cannot afford to pay eighteen pounds per bottle for a wine which was offered for sale a few years ago at fifteen shillings per bottle in old money. In short, it took me, when I read it, on a world-wide wine tour, taught me an immense amount I had not known before and gave me a vinous interest to add to all the other travel interests of someone who has always considered travelling to be the greatest joy and to whom the sound of a ship's siren or an aircraft revving up is like a well-chilled glass of Monsieur Daniel Querre's *Blanc de Blanc cuvée privée* – the elixir of life itself.

I honestly believe that with it the least informed of us can acquire enough simply-given information to provide them with a basic working knowledge of the wines they may expect to encounter from the Cape to Czechoslovakia, so that, when glancing down what might otherwise be a totally unintelligible wine list, they are enabled by this book to recognize a wine or two on which Johnnie has particularized and therefrom to embark upon a tasting with, as it were, his guiding hand upon the bottles.

If there are any who read this book who feel inclined to ask the rhetorical question 'Why all this fuss about a glass of wine?' I will make my husband's answer, for it represents to me the most charming, acceptable, and profound comment upon this pleasure . . . *'Wine, which irons out the creases in our daily lives.'*

In conclusion, which is a nice discretion – for which I am certainly not at all famous! – I would like to share with you a little quote of Rabelais which, in its original French, overhangs the entrance to our kitchen doors. *Le plaisir de la table est de tous les âges. Il s'associe à tous les autres et reste le dernier, lorsque l'âge a fait disparaître les autres.*

We have it in French, because the English are, in the main, not very good at foreign languages and thus we may possibly avoid offending the more easily offendable of our guests and friends. For the rest of you – read on, if you wish, to our somewhat free, but we think succinct, translation. . . . .

The pleasures of the table are the only ones in which man (or woman) may indulge three times a day *every* day of their lives.

FANNY CRADOCK

WINEGLASSES

One of the many laws laid down by so-called 'experts' concerns the type of wineglass to be used for each category of wine. This, like so many other edicts, is not only calculated to frighten people off wine drinking, but is also unnecessary.

Of course the wineglass is 'important' if you aim to extract every scrap of pleasure from your wines, but I must stress that you do not have to spend much, or have a vast and varied collection.

All you ever need, to serve the finest wines to the greatest connoisseurs, is an ordinary 'tulip glass' (No. 6 in my diagrams). It is so named because the bowl is wider in the middle than at top and bottom, like me. The best and most usual size is a $6\frac{2}{3}$ oz one. However, I have set the full range out for your inspection in case you should want to build up a classic collection.

The only cardinal rule is that all glass should be plain and clear; never cut, coloured or even slightly tinted except for the stems of Hock glasses. All good 'tulip'-shaped glasses should have stems which are approximately the same length as their bowls and these must be well balanced.

There are two pleasures in wine drinking – apart from the taste – 'colour' and 'bouquet, nose or smell'. Studying the varying shades is a very definite pleasure which it would be impossible to enjoy if the glasses were themselves coloured or patterned; the former changes the wine colours and the latter distorts them. Appreciating the scent is impossible if it all disperses before you can sniff and enjoy it, so you must have a glass which is *narrower at the top* than in the middle to preserve this 'nose'.

Incidentally – something English wine waiters seem to have forgotten – glasses should never be more than half filled so that the wine may be swirled around without it spilling. This movement helps to bring out or develop that smell or 'nose'. It therefore follows that you need a fairly large glass if you are to be able, correctly, to offer your guests a reasonable amount of wine.

Glass No. 6 in the diagrams also is a good average size for all table wines, but if you are going to extend your collection at all, fortified wines – like Port, Sherry and Madeira – being much stronger really need smaller glasses like No. 8, a 5 oz one.

When it comes to Champagne, stay perfectly correct and use your ordinary 'tulip' or buy a 'flute' (No. 5 in the diagrams). Just abstain from investing in those stupid, old-fashioned, shallow bowl glasses which, by their shape, dissipate the characteristic bubbles so carefully induced by the makers.

DIAGRAMS (pp 6 & 7)

Key:

1. Small brandy Balloon.
2. Large brandy Balloon.
3. Sherry 'taster' or 'copita .
4. Hock glass.
5. Champagne 'flute'.

6. This medium $6\frac{2}{3}$ fl oz 'tulip' is all you ever need.
7. Ideal claret glass.
8. Small 5 fl oz 'tulip' for fortified wine.
9. Large 10 fl oz 'tulip'.
10. Ideal burgundy glass.

CORKSCREWS

The origin of the corkscrew is as much a mystery as that of the *Marie Celeste*. There are countless theories, but none is substantiated by a single shred of real evidence. We do know, however, that the corkscrew made its début in the latter part of the eighteenth century. During the whole of this century it was not called a corkscrew but bore the name of 'bottle screw'. We also know that a bottle screw – almost certainly of an earlier form than the one to which we have just referred – was mentioned several times by the poet Nicholas Amherst in his book of verse *On Several Occasions*, *circa* 1720. He called it a 'bottle Scrue'.

Before any form of cork or corkscrew was in use, wine was stored in flagons and in Greek amphorae and insulated from the atmosphere by a top film of oil and then a rammed-down 'stopper' of lambswool.

What is of vital importance to us today is the kind of corkscrew we should aim to have to ensure we handle our wines with the greatest ease and gentleness. There are two main types: the ordinary one, which has a single thread, and the one which is infinitely superior, having two threads. These turn in opposite directions simultaneously. This latter type ensures corks can be drawn with great ease and in a steadier and less uncomfortable posture. The best available is *Valezina*. Whichever type you choose, however, make sure that you do not buy one of the kind with a rounded spiral because the edge is neither thin enough nor sharp enough; it therefore tends to break up the cork as it descends into it. So be certain that yours has a 'cut edge'. I cannot emphasize too strongly that money spent on cheap corkscrews is simply money thrown down the drain.

To draw the cork first cut the metal capsule *just below the rim of the bottle neck*, not on a line which is level with the top, because this metal cover is chemically treated with lead and can taint the wine by contact with it. Then take a clean napkin and wipe the neck of the bottle thoroughly and insert the corkscrew carefully, straight down the centre of the cork. Withdraw the cork with a slow, steady movement, making sure that you do not subject the bottle to jarring. The cork should be drawn several hours before service for a red wine if it is young, but an older and more delicate wine can stand very little of such exposure. The reason for allowing this breathing time is that wine is a living thing and a new activity is set up on contact of the wine with the air; even a raw young wine will mellow quite considerably. White wines need only about a quarter of an hour as a general rule – they are at their best a very short time after the cork has been drawn.

The method of drawing a Champagne cork is quite different and very few people seem to know the correct way. It is thought by the ignorant that being an expensive, celebration wine there should be a great flourish, a loud pop and that the cork should shoot through the air and either hit the ceiling or, in all probability, one of the guests; in addition to which a lot of the liquid pours out of the bottle. So they hold the bottle upright and pull the cork out or lever it out with the thumbs.

In fact there should be practically no noise and no waste of expensive wine. The correct method is to arm yourself with a clean napkin and, removing the wire and foil, wrap the napkin round the neck of the bottle. Now grip the cork firmly in one hand and hold the bottom of the bottle in the other, tilt to an angle of forty-five degrees and twist the bottle, *not* the cork, until you feel them separate. Now pour the wine slowly into the glasses.

CELLARS, CELLARAGE AND STORAGE WITHOUT CELLARS

A cellar is the perfect storage place for wines and may be situated either above or below ground; so let us consider the ideal place and the salient points which are essential to perfect conditions therein.

The cellar must be of a constant temperature with a variation of no more than two or three degrees; ideally this temperature should be between ten and thirteen degrees centigrade (50–55°F). Wherever it is situated, a wine cellar should be as dark as possible. It must also have very adequate ventilation and an atmosphere which is neither too humid nor too dry. The perfect wine cellar should be vaulted whether it is made in brick or hewn out of the living rock, and it should always face north.

Being dark, a wine cellar will need an electric light which should be from low-powered bulbs, since high-powered ones would affect the stability of the temperature. Condensation must be avoided as far as possible and, as much as is practical today, vibration should be minimal. There is a very effective method which is within the range of all of us for keeping a cellar down to the right temperature in hot weather; the floor should be spread with *river-bed* sand and this sand should be watered regularly. Racks to hold the wine bottles may be made of metal, wood, brick or concrete and if barrels are to be stored *in toto* these must rest upon low stands so shaped as to hold the barrels steadily *at all times*.

The cellars of wine producers vary tremendously. In the Champagne district of France, for example, there are many miles of underground cellars, some of which are as much as forty to fifty feet below ground level. In other areas the wine cellars are at ground level such as those in the wine lodges of Oporto (Portugal) or the great cathedral-like structures of the Jerez Bodegas (Spain).

Cellarage is the generic term for the various operations of wine production after the fermentation is finished; this naturally includes storage in correct conditions and at the ideal temperature. Then there is the 'fining' which means the clarification. There are minute particles in wine which make it cloudy. The modern method for removing them is by mechanical filtration, but the older, traditional way was to cause the particles to coagulate through the introduction of egg whites, isinglass or milk – these are merely examples of the substances that have been employed for this procedure. Another important process is 'racking', which means drawing off the wine from one barrel and transferring it to another in order to clear the wine of any lees or dregs.

Making up the ullage is also vital! 'Ullage', as applied to wines, sometimes refers to the amount of air space in a cask, or it can in trade terms mean the reverse, in which case it implies the actual liquid content. Making it up is done either by introducing more wine into the barrel, or, in France for example, the job is sometimes done by putting pebbles in to take up the excess air space. When all these things have been done the cellars are then used for the bottling, corking and 'binning', which is the placing of bottles in wine racks.

For anyone genuinely interested in wine study a few hours spent in a great cellar under the guidance of an expert is a fascinating experience. It is an education just to see the loving care which goes into the production of wines which we are then able to enjoy in prime condition and at top quality.

Unfortunately houses with cellars are rare today except for the unfortunate few who have vast cellarage under vast houses with absolutely no domestic help. The rest of us must manage as best we can. Happily for us, small stocks of wine *can* be stored without benefit of cellars, but it is well to remember that we must, even so, aim for a storage area which comes as nearly as possible within the temperature range of 10–13°C. It is also important to have a dry, dark area at our disposal.

Violent changes do affect wines seriously, so these facts *must* be borne in mind when choosing a home for your wines within your own. In most houses or flats a cupboard under the stairs or some similar position would be the best solution.

Obviously you cannot keep wines for any great length of time under these makeshift conditions, so do not contemplate buying young wines to lay down for maturing and drinking in several years' time. If you wish to do this, approach a reliable, well-established wine merchant who, you will find, will usually store the wines you buy from him and only charge you a nominal sum for storing them until you are ready to drink them.

Begin by buying one of the easily obtainable wine bins – racks – to hold the bottles. You can obtain them in almost any size ranging from ones which hold a dozen bottles, and they can be bought in triangular shapes to fit under stairs. The cost is usually very moderate.

In order to obtain adequate air circulation, put an air vent into the door of the cupboard and then bore two or more holes in an inconspicuous position low down in one of the bottom stairs, to one side of whatever stair covering you are using. A friend of mine recently bought a tiny country cottage and under the stairs he designed and made – in a surprisingly small area – a below-stairs wine cellar in miniature. It was enough to store one hundred and sixty-eight bottles!

All table wines should be stored horizontally to keep their corks moist. Make sure you have the label uppermost. If the cork dries out, air may enter the bottle and thus ruin the wine, hence these simple rulings. On the other hand, spirits *must* be stored upright – if the alcohol should come in contact with the cork for any length of time it will destroy it.

Tastes differ and I can only offer you a few guide-lines for starting your own cellar. You could hardly form any small collection without a red and a white Burgundy, a dry and a sweet white Bordeaux and one light and one more lusty Claret (red Bordeaux). You can then expand to include Loire wines, Italian red and white wines, Hocks, Moselles, Yugoslavian and Spanish red and white wines. I suggest that, apart from any small initial capital outlay which you can manage, you aim to give up one round of drinks at the 'local' or a few packets of cigarettes each week and use your savings for adding a bottle or two of wine to your modest store. This way, like savings, small beginnings will soon assume very healthy proportions.

To give you some idea I submit the following list which will satisfy many palates and provide for a great number of occasions.

APERITIFS

Dry Sherry, a Fino or a Manzanilla
Medium Sherry, an Amontillado
Dry Madeira, a Sercial
Dry White Port
Vermouth, Dry
Vermouth, Sweet

TABLE WINES

White Burgundy (dry)
White Bordeaux (dry)
Graves
White Bordeaux (sweet)
Sauternes or Barsac
Dry Moselle
Dry Hock
Dry White Italian
Red Burgundy
Red Bordeaux (Claret)
Red Italian
Champagne (non-vintage) or a dry Sparkling White Wine
Port
Brown or Cream Sherry
Bual or Malmsey Madeira

AFTER DINNER DIGESTIVES AND LIQUEURS

Cognac
Armagnac
Marc de Bourgogne
Liqueurs (to taste)

A WINE TASTING

Let me first explain how a professional wine tasting is set up and how it works and then you can adapt it to your own, possibly more modest, requirements.

The set-up may seem complex at first but it is, in fact, the reverse. In the tasting room you will need a table or series of tables, table-cloths, a row of candles and the bottles to be sampled. If possible you take a collection of short candlesticks or bottles and stick candles into them. As an alternative you can stick the candles into small, fat blobs of plasticine, pull the edges down securely on to very small plates, and then stuff in leaves to conceal the plasticine.

To support your palate and bring out the best in the wines you will also need plain, dry biscuits and little cubes of cheese. In Europe Gruyère is regarded as ideal; its poor relation Emmenthal is the second best and real English Cheddar will do very well in England, but make sure it is real and not some dreadful imitation! Thus the order will read, back row – CANDLES, next row forward – WINES, next row forward – CHEESE CUBES AND BISCUITS and finally in the front – wineglasses, ordinary standard 'tulip' glasses as explained already.

Most professional tastings are held in the morning. Professional wine tasters have coffee and dry biscuits for breakfast so that their taste-buds are fresh and unimpaired but, except perhaps for Sunday morning wine-tasting parties, this is not practical domestically. I will go through the professional tasting ritual and add those additional items that you will need, and then go on to suggest how you can 'cheat' this a little to create a pleasurable occasion and still learn a considerable amount.

No wine is swallowed by the professionals! A wooden box is filled with sawdust and placed in position in front of the table. Each taster pours out a very small quantity of wine and lifts the glass to the candlelight so as to see very clearly the colour and the clarity of the wine. With this done the 'nose' or 'bouquet' is enjoyed as the 'second pleasure'. The wine in the glass is swirled round gently and, at the risk of sounding funny in print, the nose is then stuck into the glass – so far as its shape will permit – this is how you inhale the full scent or aroma. Then comes the 'third pleasure' – the tasting of the wine. This is done by sipping on to the front of the tongue and gradually working the sip round the mouth until the whole flavour rolls over the interior of the mouth. The wine is then spat out into the sawdust; if this were not done at big serious tastings all the tasters would be paralytic before they had half finished. This is why I suggest you forget the sawdust and settle for looking, smelling, sipping, swallowing and finally comparing opinions with your friends. After this clear your palate with a little bit of biscuit or cheese and move on to the next wine. This is the way in which you can, over a series of wine tastings, select wines you like and at the price you wish to pay and thus build up a small cellar.

Never try to have too many different wines at one tasting – your palate and taste-buds will become exhausted and confused. Both will then cease to recognize and remember. Limit yourselves to a few red Burgundies or Clarets and thus give yourself a fair chance of selecting and of remembering clearly enough to acquire that all-important quality – *a good wine memory*.

Let us assume that you wish to start a small cellar. With this in mind, give a series of tastings. *You* select the type, or types, of wine, reducing your final choice to four or five. Your selection will be governed by what you wish to determine by the experiment. Let us consider clarets in this context. On the modest scale of our think-ing in this book you would probably confine yourselves to only one or two such wines. You might indeed have decided already which particular year you wanted. Still it would remain for you to select your final choice from several shippers. Here then is a ready-made tasting, a *Château* Something shipped by Messrs Jones & Co. will be different from one shipped by Messrs Smith & Robinson.

An alternative arises if your aim in the tasting is to choose between four years of any particular type of wine perhaps between 1964 and 1967. Here is another ready-made tasting plan. Again, you may have chosen a year but still be uncertain as to which of four specific wines you want. Here lies a third tasting.

A fourth possibility arises if we ponder the extensions of this theme, perhaps a tasting of two or more groups of four different wines. In this case the order of precedence must be considered, and here arises the primary talking point of wine tasting which you will find well-nigh inexhaustible throughout your vinous studies. On this subject, opinions differ; controversies rage. We consider you would be safe to apply the same principles and to adopt the same order as you do at the table: (1) Dry white wines, (2) Clarets, (3) Burgundies, (4) Sweet white dessert wines.

These are literally the barest bones of the matter and I may well be accused of over-simplification. It *is* only the beginning. The possible divisions and subdivisions are virtually endless. Rightly or wrongly I am convinced that too much detail in the first dose, like too many wines at early tastings, will merely confuse and bewilder. It is all rather like arithmetic in relation to higher mathematics; you learn and then you proceed to unlearn. However, I do not wish you to take anything on trust from me, like those revoltingly pompous old folk who say to young people, 'that is quite enough for you to digest at your age', so I offer you, in extenuation, one 'higher mathematics' example.

Here are the wines which were chosen in consultation with the late Monsieur André L. Simon for the 1949 dinner which he subsequently described (my wife cooked, garnished and served all twelve courses at the table) as 'almost beyond belief'. The wine list is quoted in its entirety from the 1949 Summer Number of *Wine and Food*, the gastronomic quarterly edited by M. Simon.

Marcharnudo Fino
Meursault Charmes 1942
Wehlener Sonnenuhr Auslese 1943
Château Haut-Brion 1934
Château Haut-Bailly 1929
Château d'Yquem 1937
Taylor's 1924
Roullet and Delamain 1906 Grande Champagne

In the above, the sherry led to a white Burgundy; but the character of the year younger Moselle was so highly developed that it was able to follow its senior successfully. Both the ensuing clarets were aristocrats; the former, *Haut-Brion*, is of a greater classification than the latter, *Haut-Bailly*, which nevertheless took precedence in this outstanding year – 1929. *Château d'Yquem* is the greatest of all the Sauternes, after which came the very fine port and lastly the Cognac of another glorious year. It was quite a dinner.

THE WINES OF FRANCE

France is, without doubt, the most important wine-producing country in the world, so, although in this book the lower-priced wines must take pride of place, no serious student would be happy if I failed to deal in some detail with the greatest areas and their products. I will therefore divide this chapter into regions starting with:

BORDEAUX

Red Wines

It is without argument that the Bordeaux region of France produces a greater quantity of red wine of the highest quality and in far greater variety than any other part of the country. The annual output is in the region of two hundred and thirty million bottles.

Red Bordeaux or 'claret' is often described as the Queen of Wines, being, as the great André Simon said, 'Like the perfect wife. Claret looks nice; is natural and wholesome; is ever helpful, yet not assertive; dependable always! gracious and gentle, but neither dumb, dull nor monotonous! a rare gift and a real joy.'

The more ordinary clarets can be drunk with pleasure when quite young, say three to four years old, but the higher-quality ones age and last better in bottle than any other table wine. By far the greatest quantity is shipped in barrel and bottled in the country to which it is exported; these bulk shipments enable the wine to be sold at a much lower price, but the best of the production is bottled in its own *château* and thus commands a higher price. The *château*-bottled wines have the words '*Mis en Bouteille au Château*' printed on the label, together with the name of the *château*. The year of the vintage and the name of the *château* are also stamped on the cork.

The main area of production is the Médoc region on the left bank of the Gironde river. This starts about five miles north of Bordeaux and ends near the mouth of the Gironde. This is subdivided into Haut-Médoc – the southern part from which come all the greatest wines – and the Bas-Médoc (or, as it is now termed, just Médoc) which in the main supplies the *Vins Ordinaires*.

In 1855 the wines of the *Médoc Châteaux* were officially graded into growths. There are four 1st growths and their names are *Château Lafite-Rothschild, Château Latour, Château Margaux* and *Château Haut-Brion*. The last, although it comes from the Graves district, was considered so outstanding that it was included with the Médoc wines. There follow fifteen 2nd growths, fourteen 3rd growths, ten 4th growths and eighteen 5th growths; after these come four *Crus Exceptionels* and some two hundred *Crus Bourgeois Supérieurs*. It is among these latter wines that, due to the enormous increase in prices, many excellent wines are being discovered which had not even been considered heretofore. This 1855 classification has never been altered and while it has stood the test of time very well indeed it is generally agreed that some changes could well be made now. The outstanding claimant for upgrading is *Château Mouton Roth-schild*, which is at the head of the 2nd growths and well deserves the distinction of being classified as a 1st growth. Its original exclusion has been the cause of bitter rivalry between the two branches of the Rothschild family, one of which owns *Château Lafite* and the other *Château Mouton*. There are several 3rd, 4th and 5th growths which, in my opinion, and I am far from alone in this, well merit promotion; there are also some which should be demoted and replaced by certain of the *Bourgeois Supérieurs* group.

When you come to analyse the wines of the Médoc you discover that the further south you go, the more light and delicate these wines become. This, of course, is a mere generalization and, as always, there are exceptions. The area is so vast and the wines so innumerable that I shall restrict myself to an analysis of the more renowned areas while pausing to remind you that there are also many good 'small' growths in these areas, in the hope that you will be interested enough to sample many of them over the ensuing years.

If you set out from the town of Bordeaux to make a tour of the Haut-Médoc you will, at the onset, travel through a number of villages whose production of red Bordeaux comes under the modest but sound categories of *Cru Bourgeois Supérieur* and *Cru Bourgeois*. Among these you will catch your first glimpse of *Château La Lagune* from Ludon, *Château Senejac* from Le Plan-Médoc and an excellent 5th growth *Château Cantemerle* from Macau; this latter being specially interesting because it is as good as a great many of the 3rd and 4th growths. *Château La Tertre* is also an outstanding 5th growth coming from Arsac and I would likewise commend to you a 3rd growth called *Château Giscours* which comes from Labarde.

This tour will bring you to the outskirts of Margaux where you will find such treasures as Cantenac's *Château Brane-Cantenac*, a 2nd growth, and the three *château* wines of *Kirwan, D'Issan* and *Palmer*. This trio are all in the 3rd growth category. Then come the wines of Margaux – elegant, delicate and having a far more distinguished bouquet. The greatest of these, as you might imagine, is the *Château Margaux* itself, which is often called 'Le Roi du Médoc', although I am of the opinion that this wine possesses so many feminine qualities that it should be called 'La Reine'. Indeed, one of my greatest memories is having found in the private cellars of Château Loudenne, a *Château Margaux* 1875, which, of course, was pre-phylloxera and a very great vinous experience.

Coming back into the realms of current and future wine experiences which are available to us all, there are in this region four 2nd growths which I would commend to you. *Châteaux Lascombes, Rausan-Segla, Rausan Gassies* and *Durfort*. To these you must add four 3rd growths – *Malescot Sainte-Exupéry, Ferrière, Desmirail* and *Marquis d'Alesme-Becker* – and also a very good 4th growth called *Marquis de Terme*. If you then head north the next district of some importance which you will encounter is St. Julien where the wines are still light and delicate but with a shade more body to them than those of Margaux. In this St. Julien region, I hope you will agree when you taste them, among the best are the 2nd growth wines *Leoville-Lascases, Leoville-Poyferré, Leoville-Barton, Ducru-Beaucaillou* and one of my very great favourites *Gruaud-Larose*. Also in this region are two 3rd growths *Lagrange* and *Langoa-Barton* and three 4th growth category wines carrying the names *Branaire-Ducru, Talbot* and *Beychevelle*.

Thus we come to Pauillac, the most important district of all; it

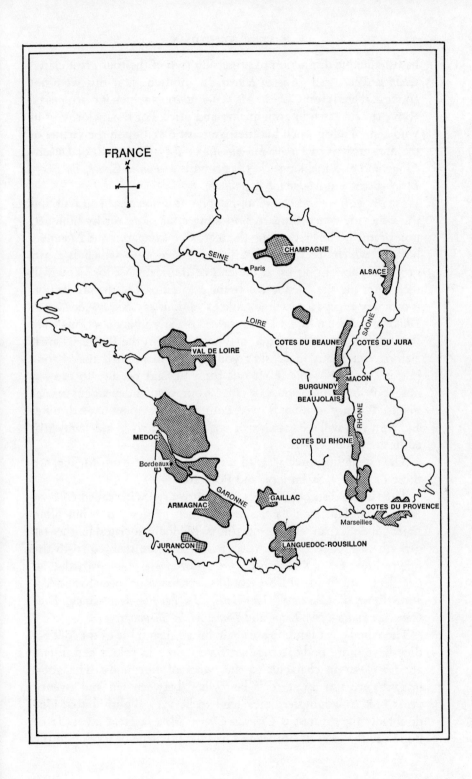

has the unique distinction of possessing two of the four great clarets *Château Lafite* and *Château Latour*. In addition, as if this were not enough, there is too *Château Mouton-Rothschild* which is often placed above the first two in both quality and price. For the majority of us who cannot afford such luxuries we must dwell upon the virtues of the 2nd growth of *Pichon-Longueville* or the 4th growth of *Duhart-Milon* and also include such 5th growths as *Pontet-Canet, Batailley, Lynch-Bages* and *Mouton d'Armailhacq*.

Finally you will reach Sainte-Estephe. It is here that you will find the wines are much sturdier, possessing a far more earthy bouquet, nose or smell. The best among them are *Cos d'Estournel* and *Montrose*, both of which are 2nd growths, and *Calon-Segur* which is a 3rd growth. These bring us to the end of the Haut-Médoc. You will then enter the Bas-Médoc where the greatest part of the production is ordinary except for such notable exceptions as *Châteaux Loudenne, Laujac* and *Livran*. What I suggest you do, if you are a serious wine student, is to embark upon a small tour through the Bordeaux area. Before you begin make sure you have a map, then make your journey, in the sequence set out for you, and be sure to carry a notebook in which you can enter your own independent assessments. When your tour is over, compare your opinions with mine and then you will see whether or not we have arrived independently at the same conclusions.

The remaining three areas of importance, apart from Médoc, are those of Graves, St Emilion and Pomerol.

The Graves district produces a very great red wine called *Château Haut-Brion*. This is, in fact, a wine which has less body but often more finesse than any of its three Médoc associates in the 1st growth category of 1855. At its best it is more than equal to the other three. In addition there are a dozen classified growths, all excellent, and from which I would select for your special consideration those of *Châteaux Haut-Bailly, La Mission-Haut-Brion, Pape Clement, Smith-Haut-Lafite* and *Domaine de Chevalier*.

The wines of St Emilion are again lustier than those of the Médoc, they have more body strength, are very deep in colour and in fact are far closer in character to the wines of Burgundy. The good growths are usually at their best when between ten and twenty years old. As youngsters they tend to be very slightly bitter. Undoubtedly the greatest is *Château Cheval Blanc*, a great favourite of mine and the last red Bordeaux I had the privilege of serving to the late M. André L. Simon on his ninety-third birthday. It is named after an old inn called the 'Cheval Blanc' or White Horse. This is where the 'men of quality' of the region refreshed themselves in bygone days paying homage to their *suzerain* (overlord) in the town of Libourne.

Almost on a par is *Château Ausone*, produced from a vineyard planted entirely with old French vines. Some of these are over a hundred years old. Then, amongst the remainder you will, I hope, enjoy, particularly, those of *Châteaux Belair, Canon, Figeac, Pavie, Fourtet* and *Trottevieille*.

The Pomerol wines are very similar to those of St Emilion but are a little softer on the palate and possibly a shade more gracious in character. There are no outstandingly great ones amongst them, but I have always kept a supply of *Château Petrus* in my cellar. Thereby hangs a tale. In 1954 I wrote to a great friend of mine in the wine trade and asked for some good little wines to lay down for some years. Among those he recommended was *Château Petrus*. I bought several cases – I still have some left – and I paid around fifteen shillings a bottle for the 1952 vintage. About nine months ago while glancing through a restaurant wine list in London I saw this same *Château Petrus* listed at £25 per bottle; a few weeks later, when we were dining in the South of France at our absolutely favourite restaurant Le Moulin des Mougins, I told the owner, our valued friend M. Roger Vergé, this story. To my horror he laughed. Then without turning a hair he said that in France he would have to pay £50 a bottle for it and would sell it to his customers for £100, and get it! *Autres temps autres mœurs* with a vengeance.

Just to the east of Pomerol is the Fronsac district where production concentrates upon eminently sound but quite ordinary wines which resemble the bourgeois growths of the Médoc. There are, even so, a handful which soar to well above the general category – in particular the wine of *Château Rouet*.

On the right bank of the river Gironde, facing the Médoc, are the vineyards of Bourg and Blaye. Both make good reasonably priced wines, which are mostly sold as *Côtes de Bourg* or *Premières Côtes de Blaye*, but the best of the Bourg wines stem from *Châteaux Rousset, Tayac, Falfas* and *Bosquet*. From Blaye you will be rewarded by such exceptional ones as *Châteaux Bellevue, Charron, Les Foure* and *Saugeron*.

B

Every other Bordeaux area grows red wine but it is practically all of the *Vin Ordinaire* quality which, while very palatable when drunk *in situ*, is not really worth while transporting to England. It is among the 'bad travellers'.

White Wines

If you ask the average layman what is meant by the wines of Bordeaux the usual answer will be 'clarets', which is what the English have called red Bordeaux wines for many generations. The word comes from Old French, the modern French being *Clairet*. In fact, this vast region also produces the great white dessert wines of both *Sauternes* and *Barsac* and in addition yields a great range of white wines which includes both the sweet and the dry. There is another misconception here because if you try your question again, 'What is Graves?' you will undoubtedly – except among the very well informed – receive the answer 'White wine', though Graves also produces red wines which we can count as featuring among the great.

So let us begin by positioning Graves (both red and white) on the map. You will find it south of Bordeaux on the left bank of the river Garonne. Now let us analyse the *White Graves* and divide them into good wines of good value within the reach of all purses and splendid wines which are regarded by many as being very expensive. I must therefore emphasize that in the matter of all great wines the cost *must* be of secondary consideration to wine connoisseurs and should be to a wine student, but, alas, is more often not! The great ones are not the majority, as we all know, so we must understand that the bulk of the white wines of Graves represent a blending of several years, mixing the good and not so good of different vineyards and achieving wines of up to ten per cent alcoholic strength. These are then sold under the generic name *Graves* and the wines of twelve per cent and over are sold as *Graves Supérieures*. The dry ones of both *Graves* and *Graves Supérieures* are never more than fairly dry and cannot be compared with the taste of a dry white Burgundy or a wine from the Loire. Equally, the sweet white wines are light ones and not so sweet as *Sauternes*.

There are a number of *châteaux* producing higher-quality dry white Graves and these take the names of the producing *châteaux*. The best of these are *Haut-Brion, Carbonnieux, Couhins, Chevalier* and *de la Brede*, all prefixed with the word *Château*. The last named, *de la Brede*, is the showpiece of the district and the *château* itself is in fact a five-hundred-year-old medieval castle. Two hundred years ago this was the home of the great philosopher Montesquieu and his descendants are still in residence.

Between Graves and Barsac – still on the left bank of the Garonne – are three 'communes' or parishes bearing the names Cerons, Pondesac and Illats. All produce white wines, some of which are similar to dry *Graves* and some which are nearly as sweet as *Barsac* from the neighbouring district.

Next comes the Barsac area which is really a part of the Sauternes district, lying south of Bordeaux. I began my wine drinking with *Barsac* when I was very young. It was so nice and sweet, but of course I soon realized that it was by no means suitable for each and every dish; everyone must begin somewhere and then by drinking more and more wines the palate will develop and the imbiber become more perceptive.

The growers of this wine like to think that they are autonomous and quite separate from their grand connections – those elegant and famous *Sauternes*. In fact, as I have just pointed out, Barsac is a part of Sauternes and it is really just as silly as the English, Scottish and Welsh sticking separate labels on their vehicles when they travel abroad! You can judge *Barsac*'s reputation with the English by their prefix for it, 'friendly'. Well, so what? I drank friendly *Barsac* with everything when I was an uninformed schoolboy and I am not ashamed to admit it.

Beginners to wine drinking generally enjoy this humble table wine. If and when they have an opportunity to extend their vinous knowledge they generally forget it, but vinous knowledge, remember, depends entirely upon drinking a very great number of different wines and training your taste-buds and palate to recognize one from the other, in fact, to become educated. The simple, but to us costly process, of rolling a mouthful of wine round the palate and over the taste-buds teaches both you and your palate to develop taste, and therefore to develop discernment and discrimination.

If you are buying for economy, look for bottles which carry the district name only – *Barsac*. These carry no date and are just N.V. or non-vintage. Of course, if you like *Barsac* so much that you are prepared to pay a little more, you can then launch yourself into single vineyard names, and I think I would choose for you a *Château*

Liot, a *Château Lacoste* or a *Château Grillon.* Once again by present standards these are good value. If you want to climb even higher you can go for a *Château Climens* or *Château Coutet,* but do let me remind you that whichever you are buying, *Barsac* is served chilled. Moreover, being a sweet wine it responds to slightly more chilling than you would give to say a dry, white wine; so reckon to put it in the refrigerator at ordinary domestic temperature at least one and a half hours before serving and then it will be at its best, whatever it is.

Now for *Sauternes* itself. The most famous of all these wines is called *Château d'Yquem.* This is a wine of great price, but then so are many of the finest *Sauternes,* not because of the reputation they enjoy but because of the very complicated method by which the grapes are harvested. I believe you would recoil in horror from a bunch of grapes when they are ready for turning into this wine. You see, they would be mouldy!

The bunches are left on the vines until they reach a certain and precise stage of rottenness, thereby necessitating not just one harvest but many. You will appreciate that, since the stage of overripeness must be precise and exact, some will be ready to pick by a certain date while others may take considerably longer on the vines. It can in fact take up to seven weeks to complete this particular harvest. Ponder, therefore, upon the labour cost today and you will not be so surprised at the price of this wine in bottle.

It is also interesting to realize that there is nothing arbitrary about the simple fact that *Sauternes* are regarded as the finest of all sweet wines. No one is indulging in any silly wine snobbery by this. There are two very clear-cut reasons as to why *Sauternes* are so very much in the van. The soil is 'special' or 'extra' and possesses in a remarkable degree the qualities necessary for growing *Sauternes* grapes. The picking and 'pressing' combined form the second reason.

When the grapes become ripe – by our standards – a mould called *Botrytis Cinera* settles on them. The local name for this is *La Pourriture Noble,* or in English, 'the noble rot'. The minuscule roots of this 'noble rot' pierce the grapeskins in their quest for the moisture in each grape. As these distinguished bacterial blood-suckers gorge themselves, so the grape shrivels and the ratio of sugar to water intensifies, thus increasing the sweetness of the wine produced. Naturally, when the mould settles on the bunches it does so in a haphazard sort of way, singling out certain grapes on which to commence its orgy and thereby forcing that regular and repetitive harvesting so that the last of the crop is sometimes taken only just ahead of the first autumn frosts. Remember always that each time harvesting is done, only the perfectly rotten grapes are removed.

Despite all this, *Sauternes* do have one thing in common with humble *Barsac*. The very modest ones will not be 'vintage', they will merely carry the generic label *Sauternes;* will probably be made from that very last beat-the-frosts harvesting and are very inexpensive.

If you propose spending a little more I would recommend a sampling of some of the single *château*-named wines like *Château d'Arche Lapaurie, Château Guiraud, Château Filhot* or *Château Suduiraut.*

I said at the beginning that *Château d'Yquem* was the finest, the greatest and the most world-renowned of the white French table wines, but this does not mean that there are not one or two of equal greatness among the German wines, which, of course, I shall be dealing with in due course in our natural progression towards wine knowledge.

It only remains to point out here that the result of all this loving labour, carried on from father to son through untold generations, produces a white wine which can attain a very great age and go on improving for most of the time. Indeed *Yquems* have been found to be perfect after a hundred years. Of course, the colour changes over the years. In youth *Yquem* is a clear amber and in maturity it turns to old gold. The sweetness also diminishes with age. Some years ago I was fortunate enough to receive a case of the 1924 *Château d'Yquem* from the cellars of the late Lord Trenchard. I served it slightly more chilled than an average table wine and I poured it into chilled liqueur glasses. Smelling it, tasting it, drinking it, were experiences which I shall never forget, but, and this is a very important point to stress, this was an experience which came to me only once (unfortunately) throughout my long lifetime!

If you now cross the river to the right bank of the Garonne you will find Sainte-Croix-du-Mont, home of a quality of sweet white wine which is rather rare in England today, but most rewarding if you can find it. North of this is Loupiac, providing a fairly sweet white wine of which the best is undoubtedly *Château de Ricaud*. From Loupiac to Bordeaux lies the area of Premières Côtes de Bordeaux from which come fairly ordinary wines, both sweet and dry. Finally, there is a very large district which lies between the two rivers Garonne and Dordogne which is called Entre-Deux-Mers which means 'between two seas', although it should be, I suppose, 'between two rivers'. It is not my idea of an attractive table wine, but it is tonic and can be drunk by those people who cannot drink other white wines. A section of this region called Sainte-Foy-Bordeaux does, on the other hand, produce a distinctive semi-dry or sweet wine, which has some elegance. Harking back to *Entre-Deux-Mers* for a moment, it makes a good marriage with the Arcachon oysters as it does with other shellfish and shad from the river Dordogne. There is an odd thing about the service of oysters too in this area: they are generally accompanied by tiny home-made sausages. My wife is a purist about oysters. She is a passionate supporter of the dictum laid down by the late, great André L. Simon in his dictionary of gastronomy, I quote . . . 'Even a drop of lemon juice is the thin edge of the wedge of heresy.' Fanny becomes vituperative at the mere suggestion of eating any kind of sausage with any kind of oyster. The local inhabitants of this area have a motto which runs, '*Entre Deux Huîtres, Entre Deux Mers*', which, being literally translated, means 'between two oysters, between two seas', but it really suggests for every couple of oysters swallowed take a couple of mouthfuls of the local wine.

It is not possible in a book of this nature to specify particular wines of the lower growths, as the shippers are always on the hunt from year to year, particularly at the present time, to get the best value and quality for the price from both good and mediocre vintages, for even in a bad year careful searching will produce some good wines. I will, however, give you the names of Bourgeois Growth Médoc wines which I have encountered and found very drinkable:

Château Siran, Château Bellegrave, Château La Dame-Blanche, Château Lanesan, Château Meyney, Château Phelan-Segur, Château Paveil-de-Luze, Château Senejac, Château Bel-Air-Legrave, Château Laujac, Château Liversan, Château Malescot, Château de Pez, Château Les-Ormes-de-Pez and *Château Livran.*

BURGUNDY

Red Wines

Burgundy produces some of the greatest red wines in the world. As a general rule they have more body and are more robust, in fact more masculine, than the wines of Bordeaux and are therefore referred to as the 'Kings of Wine'. It is, however, a mistake to imagine that Burgundy is always heavy, for many of this region's wines possess great delicacy and are quite light. There is an old saying that red Bordeaux wines increase longevity while Burgundies encourage *l'amour*.

The production of Burgundy is much smaller than that of Bordeaux – actually about one-tenth in fine wines. Consequently it is logical to expect that the prices are also higher. One of the great differences between these magnificent wine areas is that whereas there are many imposing *châteaux* in Bordeaux with large vineyards attached, in Burgundy there are very few great estates. Most of the land is divided into small, individually owned vineyards or fields, known in France as *Climats*. Even these are very frequently subdivided so that you need not be startled to find two or more different wines deriving from one vineyard. It all depends on the particular ideas of the owner as to when to start picking the grapes or whether to pick out the under- or overripe grapes or to leave them hanging on the vines.

The general name for an estate is *Domaine*, which is the equivalent to *château* in Bordeaux. So, on the labels of the best Burgundian wines you will find the statement . . . *'Mis en Bouteille au Domaine'* (bottled on the estate).

The main red wine area is known as the Côte d'Or. This stretches from just south of Dijon right down to Chagny. It is divided into the Côte de Nuits – beginning at Fixin and ending at Nuits St Georges – and the Côte de Beaune which runs from Corton to Santenay.

From Côte de Nuits comes a chain of golden vinous names for what are considered to be the finest red wines in the world *Chambertin, Chambolle-Musigny, Grands Echézeaux, Clos de Vougeot* and above all *Vosne-Romanée* to which, very rightly, odes have been written.

While the Côte de Beaune cannot match these outstanding wines with the possible exception of Corton, this area does produce many very excellent wines of high character and quality, for instance *Beaune, Volnay* and *Pommard*. They mature earlier, are lighter in character and lower in price, so on all counts are to be recommended.

Having made what, at most, I can best describe as a cursory survey of the red wines of Burgundy I now want you to join me for a tour through the region so that we can begin to particularize.

We will launch ourselves at Dijon so that in a very few miles of motoring we will enter the Côte d'Or and make our first encounter in the village of Fixin with some of the fine wines of the Côte de Nuits. Here among a general tasting of great red Burgundies we will have our first great experience with the *Clos de la Perrière*. This big full-bodied wine must not be missed and on a tour of this region it must always be included.

Our next stop will be at Gevrey-Chambertin. Its original name was Gevrey only, but in 1847 it was incorporated and hyphenated with the name of the very great vineyard of Chambertin. There are two top quality *Chambertins* carrying just this name, the *Gevrey-Chambertin* and its neighbour the *Clos de Bèze*.

These are great rumbustious, lusty wines, rich in flavour and with what we call enormous staying power. In other words they have a great life in bottle and should never be drunk when they are young. *Chambertin* was Napoleon's favourite Burgundy, which showed that even that tiresome Corsican peasant certainly knew something about wine appreciation. Among the other very excellent wines of this region you should make a note of *Charmes-Chambertin, Chapelle-Chambertin* and *Griotte-Chambertin;* but as there are so many other distinctive wines in this area I open myself to the accusation that I am being unfair in particularizing with my 'trio'.

Next in our journey comes the village of Morey-St-Denis. Here we find several wines in the top category, very similar in character to *Chambertin* but with perhaps a shade less robustness, replacing this with more grace and flexibility. The foremost pair are *Clos de Tart* and *Clos de Lambrays*. The vineyards of these two are in the possession of single owners who tend their vines and cherish the resultant wines exactly as their predecessors have done for many centuries. On the other hand we must not forget *Bonnes Mares* which when it is at its best is a much softer wine, although you must watch out here because it varies considerably and there are several owners. Adjacent to it is Chambolle-Musigny. In addition most of the *Bonnes Mares* vineyards are to be found in the same territory. Once again the wine is a little more delicate and its flavour spreads and lingers in the mouth. The greater part of these vineyards are owned by Count Georges de Vogüë. His is a very old and distinguished family. Count Robert owns that great Champagne house of Möet et Chandon, while yet another member of the family concerns himself with *Veuve Cliquot*. After this brief parenthesis let us return to the vineyards of Burgundy. At the head of the region is *Les Musigny* and in order of discussion is hotly pursued by *Les Amoureuses* and *Les Charmes* in quality. You will also find that this area places a very great deal of *Chambolle-Musigny* on the same level; but this varies considerably according to the ideas and tastes of the shipper. You can say as a generalization that it is usually very reliable.

This is where you will come into the Vougeot area and will see the great old Château Clos de Vougeot. This *château* is the headquarters of the largest of the wine orders, the Confrérie des Chevaliers du Tastevin. This is where my wife and I were installed as Chevaliers of the order in 1951 on the occasion of the four-hundredth anniversary of the *château*. At the end of a meal of eighteen courses and thirty-six complementary wines, a little snack which lasted from 6.30 p.m. to 2 a.m., we were initiated.

The French themselves have such a high opinion of *Clos de Vougeot* that even as far back as the days of Napoleon one of his commanders, Colonel Bisson, when on his way to join the Emperor at Marengo (from where Poulet Marengo obtained its name), halted his regiment opposite the *château* and made the entire regiment present arms. We have it on good authority that today any body of troops passing the *château* makes the same gesture of homage. I would hope, of course, that you are more fortunate than we and could witness this when in the area.

Just south of Vougeot you will come to Flagey. This is a great favourite of mine, for my palate tells me that the greatest wine it produces is among the finest of all Burgundies. Alas, the name is *Grands Echézeaux*. I say alas because countless wine waiters have told me that customers will not order it in English restaurants because they find the name too difficult to pronounce and as you well know the English embarrass easily. Try saying it as I have spelt it to make the sounds: ESH-EZ-ERR. Then you will earn the respect of the wine waiter and win yourself a memorable vinous experience.

Next door to these vineyards is *Vosne-Romanée*, generally regarded as the greatest of all red wines. The bouquet of this Grand Seigneur among wines has a strange, spicy sweetness, the wine on the palate slips down while caressing the palate, and if you ever have the privilege of drinking it I will undertake that you will never forget it. This, incidentally, was the scene of my most cherished encounter between my wife and the cook/proprietress of a tiny shack restaurant in this area which enjoyed a fantastic reputation. We stopped the car outside and standing in the crude doorway, or perhaps I should say fitting into the crude doorway, was a gargantuan female, her size exaggerated by the white overall in which she was upholstered. My wife approached her and after greeting her said in French, for Madame spoke no English, 'We have heard of your reputation, Madame, please may we see the menu?' Her eyes flashed, she folded her arms across her vast bosoms, she pulled herself up to her full height and practically shouted, '*Madame, le menu ici n'existe pas, c'est moi qui est le menu*' (I am the menu). We had a gorgeous feast and ultimately became very great friends.

One of the wines of Vosne-Romanée which we drank at that luncheon-in-a-shack was the magnificent and unbeatable *Romanée-Conti*, but I would hate you to miss either of the two which followed close behind, that exquisite pair called *Richebourg* and *La Tâche*.

We near the end of this part of the tour with the last of the Côte de Nuits parishes called Nuits-Saint-Georges, a name standing for a big, robust, but not really heavy wine. The more ordinary ones are sold under the generic name of the town; but there are several which I believe you might like me to single out for your attention: *Le Saint Georges, Les Cailles, Aux Boudots* and *Les Vaucrains*.

Our next move is southwards into the second part of the Côte d'Or. Just to confuse us this is called the Côte de Beaune. We enter the first village – Aloxe – whose best vineyard is undoubtedly Corton and here you will find that very splendid wine *Le Corton*, which is the only one that can really rank alongside the greatest of all the *Côte de Nuits*.

There are two adjacent villages here, Ladoix-Serriguy and Pernand-Vergelesses. Both produce a great deal of good wine for which permission has been granted for it to be sold under the labels *Corton* or *Aloxe-Corton*.

Thus we enter Savigny-les-Beaune. The best wines from here are

Les Vergelesses, Les Marconnets and *Les Jarrons.* These are all pale in colour, soft and rather lighter than the more northerly Burgundies. Then comes the great peak of this particular journey – Beaune itself – an ancient walled city in which we find the fabulous hospital called Les Hospices de Beaune. This was founded as long ago as 1443 by a man called Nicolas Rolin and his wife. Its maintenance was assured by the Rolins who bequeathed to the hospital all the revenues from their vineyards. Since then other benefactors have donated further similar revenues to ensure maintenance continuation.

Every year on the third Sunday in November these 'Hospices' wines are sold by public auctions. They are so eagerly sought after that buyers come into Beaune from all over the world for this annual occasion. They crowd the little town, they fill the hotels and they spread out wherever they can into the surrounding villages in quest of bed and board. As a result of the highly competitive buying, combined with the pursuance of the Rolins' donation pattern, some of the best of the Côte region is offered up for sale. The resultant yield to the hospital is prodigious. It is because of this annual sale that the hospital can offer some of the most up-to-date treatment and buy the most modern equipment available at any time.

Among the wines from Beaune which merit your most close attention are *Les Grèves, Les Fèves, Clos des Mouches* and *Clos-de-la-Mousse.* If we go further down the scale I must include the generic names of *Beaune* and *Côte de Beaune.*

When at last you leave this great little town, which frankly I always do with the greatest possible reluctance, I would like you to fork right in order to come to Pommard. This is a name which is known all over the world. The wine is almost always sold under the simple label – *Pommard* – and is a straightforward, honest wine which does not possess much subtlety. Pommard is next-door neighbour to Volnay where once again a large proportion is sold under the name *Volnay.* However, by paying a very little more you can obtain wines with their own vineyard names such as *Les Caillerets, Les Champans, Les Fremiets* and lower down the scale *Les Angles, Carelle-sous-la-Chapelle, En Chevret* and *Le Clos des Chênes.* All have the true rich Burgundy flavour and are very fresh on the taste-buds.

After our visit to Volnay we leave behind us the main red Burgundy vineyards and enter the region of the white Burgundies. It is, however, well worth your while to continue the tour because, in addition to the white wines, you will also find some very sound and delightful reds as you explore. Your first will be discovered at the village of Auxey-Duresses. Keep a sharp look-out for the best vineyards here, Les Duresses, and for Meursault, whose vineyards produce a red wine called *Volnay-Santenois*.

In due course you may be as surprised as I was to discover that Chassagne-Montrachet makes some extremely good red wine of which the best known is *Clos-Saint-Jean* while the adjacent village of Santenay produces a deep red one, a little sweeter than the majority around here and called *Les Gravières*.

We are, of course, now in southern Burgundy, heading towards the Côte Chalonnaise where the wines of the northern end are sold as *Côte de Beaune Villages* and those of the southern end as *Mercurey and Givry*. They are all sound but relatively undistinguished.

This leads us to the wine of Mâcon known as *Mâcon Rouge* and produced in very large quantities. *Mâcon Rouge* is a very good *Vin du Pays* – not as lively as *Beaujolais*, but very drinkable. Moreover it is sold at an extremely reasonable price. Now as we move on yet again we begin to see ahead of us the vast area of Beaujolais. Beaujolais is the district in the south of Burgundy facing the right bank of the river Saône and spreading from Romaneche-Thorins in the Saône-et-Loire to below Villefranche in the Rhône Département. Not to be confused, please, with Villefranche on the Côte d'Azur.

Beaujolais produces red wines in great quantity and of a lightish character but has become so popular all over the world that the demand far exceeds available supplies. Please do not buy from unreliable sources. The ordinary *Beaujolais* sold under its generic name is less expensive than other Burgundies chiefly because, unlike the others, it does not improve with age and therefore does not have to be kept for five years and upwards. Even here, though, there are classifications from *Beaujolais-Villages* to *Beaujolais Supérieur* down to just plain *Beaujolais*. In fact it is very drinkable in twelve months and at its best up to about four years bottle age. There is a vogue at the moment for *Beaujolais de l'Année* which is brought over here with a great annual flourish of trumpets, towards the end of November and in the year of the vintage. In a good year this is very palatable, but it can be pretty awful in my opinion and is just not worth all the fuss and bother expended upon it. *Beaujolais* is normally served at room temperature. Nowadays many people in this country, including myself, prefer it slightly chilled as it is drunk in France, its country of origin.

There are many other *Beaujolais* and the best are sold under the names of their villages, the most notable being *Moulin-à-Vent, Fleurie, Juliénas, Morgon, Brouilly, St Amour* and *Romaneche-Thorins.* They need maturing for five to six years.

Beaujolais is practically all produced from the Gamay grape and the vines are pruned in a distinctive shape which closely resembles a five-branched candelabra. If you are passing through this district on your way to the south, stop off and taste some *Beaujolais* in its own home. You will find in each village a cellar where the growers set out their wines for you to try and among them you are almost certain to find interest for both mind and palate.

White Wines

The dry white wines of Burgundy are of finer quality and have more distinction than you will find anywhere else in the world. Other parts of France have many excellent light, dry white wines, but none of them have the body, the breeding or the bouquet of the white Burgundies.

The northernmost district – about halfway between Paris and Dijon – in the Yonne Département gives us the best known wine *Chablis,* this is dry on the palate, pale golden in colour, light, clean and free from acidity. It makes the ideal marriage with oysters, white fish and white meats.

Unfortunately, like *Beaujolais,* the demand is so great nowadays that this far exceeds the supply. The authorities have therefore decreed that genuine *Chablis* may only be sold in France under four labels: (1) *Chablis Grand Cru* or *Grands Chablis,* (2) *Chablis Premier Cru,* (3) *Chablis,* (4) *Petit Chablis* or *Bourgogne des Environs de Chablis.* However, the sad fact is that the French have no control over the name *Chablis* outside their own country, so I must warn you once again to be very careful when buying these wines and to put yourself in the hands of a really trustworthy wine merchant.

Under the first heading I think you will find that the best are *Grenouilles, Les Clos, Blanchot, Valmur* and *Vaudesir.* Under the second heading there are about a dozen names like *Chablis-Mont de Milieu, Forêts* and *Beauroy* in which you can repose your confidence. The third group cannot use a vineyard name and so merely carries the plain *Chablis* mark, while the fourth simply states on the label *Petit Chablis*.

Moving south of Dijon you will then come to the Côte d'Or. The northern part of this area produces very little white wine, but if you can lay your hands on any that bear the names *Clos de Vougeot, Musigny* or *Morey-St Denis* go for them and ensure for yourself a truly memorable wine experience.

From Beaune itself comes an excellent full-bodied wine called *Clos des Mouches*. Then continuing south you will reach *Corton-Charlemagne*. This is an outstanding wine, big, with a slightly steely taste and a flavour that lingers delectably on the palate, a wine I do not believe you will forget after sampling just once.

Next in our southerly progress comes *Meursault*, very pale in colour with a distinctive greeny tinge, but although this is a very dry wine it is much more mellow than most white Burgundies and to my mind is best when married to a fairly richly sauced fish dish.

Probably next to *Chablis* the most universally known is *Montrachet*, a lovely, powerful wine which Alexandre Dumas said should be drunk alone, kneeling and with bared head. This is a slight exaggeration, of course, but *Montrachet* does need such food as shellfish, poultry or veal to enable it to give of its best. The finest of all is just called *Le Montrachet*; incidentally the 't' is not pronounced, therefore it sounds as though it should be spelt 'Montrachet'. On a slightly lower level there are *Bâtard-Montrachet, Chevalier-Montrachet* and *Puligny-Montrachet* – in that order.

Below this are a number of villages making sound but undistinguished wines of a far lighter character, and then between Chalon and Mâcon a large quantity of wine is produced which is sold all over the world under the labels *Mâcon Blanc Supérieur* or *Mâcon Blanc*. These are lower-priced wines than the rest I have mentioned. Like these they are less dry than *Chablis*, but still smooth and fairly strong. In this district you will also find one wine which is as good as any of the Burgundies, *Pouilly-Fuissé*. This is the wine that I produced for my wife at my then favourite restaurant, now alas defunct, on the first occasion on which she consented to have luncheon with me. We never looked back.

Like *Chablis* the demand has outstripped the supply, so again great care is needed to ensure that you are not misled. I suggest you go for one of those which bears a vineyard name, such as *Château de Fuissé, Le Clos, Les Charmes, Le Paradis* or *Le Mont Garcin*.

Finally, in the lower price group look out for *Beaujolais Blanc*, very little known over here where the name *Beaujolais* is generally taken to be a synonym for a good sound red wine. This white one also has character, a strong flavour of the grape and a fair amount of body.

THE RHÔNE

The Rhône valley vineyards run from just south of Lyon to Avignon. By far the most outstanding characteristic of the wines produced here is their stability and their long-keeping quality in bottle. As they are very slow to mature they are very often not bottled for four or five years and then their bottle-life just goes on and on. It is, of course, a general tragedy today that a great many wines are drunk far too young. This does not enable the slow developers to reach their prime, but then wine consumption goes up every year and a relatively small proportion is laid down nowadays to give it a fair chance of coming to its proper maturity. This is particularly the case in the Rhône and though it sounds mad, today it is a fact that during the nineteenth century fully matured Rhône wines were frequently offered after dinner as an alternative to port.

Their northernmost district is the Côte Rôtie (Roasted Coast) and from here come the finest of the *Côte du Rhône* red wines. Côte Rôtie is divided into two separate parts, the Côte Brune and the Côte Blonde. If we speculate about the origins of these definitions it seems very likely that they were so called because of the contrasting proportions of lime in the respective soils, but there are tales that they were so named after two daughters of a former vineyard owner. I must, however, warn you that while the better sound *Côte du Rhône* wines are good, they do have the reputation for being a little unreliable.

Working southwards again we come to Condrieu and here you will find an exceptionally fine golden wine called *Château Grillet*. This is considered one of the best wines in France, but, alas, the production is very small and therefore it is almost always in short supply, but if you can find some pray do not pass it by.

Next comes the sleepy little town of Tain-l'Hermitage. Just outside the town is a vineyard with a little chapel which was given in 1225 to a returning Crusader, Henri de Sterimberg, as a reward for his heroic services. He eventually settled down there and began producing a dry white wine which is still being produced to this day. It was, as it is today, named after him, *Le Chevalier de Sterimberg*. Nor must we forget the red wines of this area; the *Hermitage* red is a finely bred strong wine with a faint aroma of honeysuckle. Close by to *Hermitage* is *Croze-Hermitage*; this red wine is a little more modestly priced, but then as you would expect it is not quite as good as *Hermitage* itself.

Opposite there is a little line of villages all of which sell the wines from their vineyards under the name of *St Joseph*. They can be very good, but once again they do not have the reliability of *Hermitage*. I would single out for special attention here the southerly village of Cornas, whose red wine is quite sound and clean, generally to be found on local wine lists in hotels and restaurants.

Let us proceed from this area now to between Orange and Avignon. Our destination is Châteauneuf-du-Pape, where the grapes grow in most unusual conditions. If you look at a sweep of vines you will see that they are thrusting up among large stones and ones which can truly be described as boulders. It is maintained that the great quality of *Châteauneuf-du-Pape* is provided by these stones. They heat up in the sun. Their heat diminishes very slowly and therefore they really act as a night-time hot-water bottle for the vines.

The red wine is heady, warm, invigorating and has great strength of flavour, but if you can run to it try for some of the better growths like *Château Vaudieu, Fortia, La Gardine, Domaine de la Nerthe, Clos de l'Oratoire des Papes* and *St Patrice*. Nor can I abstain from urging you before you leave this area to sample the far lesser-known white *Châteauneuf-du-Pape*. This is a glowing, deep golden wine, it has a steely aroma and flavour, but despite this is lusty and full of body. About ten miles away you will also find the vineyards of Gigondas. The wines produced from these vines are similar to *Châteauneuf-du-Pape* and very good drinking, but it is nevertheless slightly inferior in quality.

Finally, we go to Tavel. This produces the best of the rosés and although they are all light, frivolous and forgotten-as-soon-as-drunk, *Tavel Rosés* do have more character than any other rosé wines.

ALSACE

The wines of Alsace have never achieved the acclaim to which they are entitled. They have been recognized since the early Christian era and in the Middle Ages were exported all over Europe; but it was not until the end of the First World War and the end of the German occupation that they really had a chance to come into their own. The Germans had endeavoured to eradicate anything French and they prohibited the sale under the name of Alsatian wines. But ever since 1919 the growers have worked devotedly to improve the quality of their wines.

Alsace is a long, narrow area of very fertile land starting north of Strasbourg and stretching down to just south of Mulhouse. The Vosges mountains form a natural protection from the cold winds and gales coming in westwards and all the vineyards are situated on the west side of the river Ill which runs right down the centre.

Practically all Alsatian wines are white and approximately two-thirds of the cultivation is from the commoner types of grape. These produce a rather sharp white wine which is drunk while still very young. It is unsuitable for export but *in situ* blends very well with such basic Alsatian dishes as sauerkraut and pickled, boiled or roast pig.

The better wines, which comprise the other third of the overall production, are made from five types of grape and are normally sold under the names of these grapes.

There is *Sylvaner*, light, dry and fresh. It has little bouquet and again should be drunk while young. It does, however, make an excellent aperitif or light luncheon wine. Then there is *Riesling*, probably the most distinguished of these wines. This ages very well, is dry, delicate and fragrant and is particularly good with fish.

Do not be misled by the word *Muscat*, which usually conjures up a vision of sweet dessert wine. This, the third Alsatian variety, is dry, very fruity and makes a notable marriage with all forms of shellfish.

Traminer, although fairly dry, has a rich, lasting flavour and very distinctive nose. It will blend with highly seasoned dishes and also with white meat. In good years a *Gewurtztraminer* is produced from late-picked Traminer grapes; the result is a rather rich, full-bodied wine, not sweet but capable of being drunk with fairly sweet dishes.

Lastly there is *Tokay*, made from the Pinot grape which has nothing in common with the Hungarian *Tokay*. It is difficult to find. The production is very limited, but it more than justifies the effort expended in finding it, as I consider this wine to be the most versatile of all this series and, in fact, have served it with great success throughout a meal.

If you ever visit this region go to the house of Hugel which, with its vineyards, is situated outside the town of Riquewihr. Hugel's has remained under the control of the Hugel family for eleven generations. Each successive generation has not just maintained the quality of their wine, but made great efforts towards improving the quality.

Even if you are not a great wine enthusiast a tour of this part of France is well worth while, for you will eat and drink extremely well and also see some most beautiful examples of medieval architecture, in spite of the devastation wrought by two modern wars. The town of Riquewihr is the best preserved of any and is enchanting.

CHAMPAGNE

Champagne, the greatest of all sparkling wines, is so far beyond the price reach of the majority of people nowadays that a lengthy study of it would not be justified in a book of this nature. If I just explain how it is made, quite shortly, you may at least be able to understand why it is so costly. In addition there are many sparkling wines made by the Champagne Method and the same explanation will put you in the picture over these.

Wine has been made in Champagne from the most ancient times, but although greatly appreciated and sought after by the privileged classes of those bygone days, the wines were still red ones until late in the seventeenth century. Then about 1668 the Champenois, always striving for perfection, discovered how to produce a very delicate white wine. They also found that a second fermentation took place in the bottle as the weather got warmer in summer and that the wine became effervescent.

The pioneers of the Champagne Method, by which the fermentations were regulated and the sparkle retained, were a Benedictine monk called Dom Perignon and the monks of Hautvillers Abbey.

In order that you may appreciate the reasons for the superb virtues of Champagne I will take you right through the process.

Harvesting usually begins in the second half of September. The date is fixed annually, by official decree and after laboratory tests for sugar content and acidity. The 'pickers' cut the bunches of grapes and heap them into baskets. These are taken by 'porters' to the end of the line where the grapes are turned on to wicker trays and examined by the 'sorters' who throw out any unripe, spoiled or squashed ones. The good ones are then placed in large wicker baskets (caques) holding about 150 lb apiece. The 'loaders' put these on to well-sprung trucks and only then are they conveyed to the presses. This is all done with the greatest possible care to ensure that none of the good grapes are damaged.

The 'pressing' is a very delicate procedure too, for it is necessary to obtain a 'white' wine from a preponderance of 'black' grapes. Therefore the juice must never be tainted in colour by contact with the skins. The pressing therefore, has to be rapid, taking a mere one and a half to two hours for three quick actions. The juice thus obtained is called the *cuvée* and it forms the basis for the great Champagnes. It flows into large casks and is then poured into other casks (purifiers) where it rests for about twelve hours so that the pips, skins and other impurities can settle. After this settling process, the juice is drawn off into casks which are then transported to the cellars.

Then comes the first fermentation at a constant temperature of 22°C (72°F). As the fermentation works, so it bubbles tumultuously. This continues for several days and only then begins to diminish until it ceases altogether at the end of about three weeks. It is then racked (drawn off to clear it from dregs or lees) for the first time, exposed to a colder temperature and then drawn off again.

Early in the new year, one of the most important operations begins – the benlding of various growths (crus). Each different Champagne producer blends to his own particular taste, this remains constant year after year. In early spring the 'still' wine is drawn off into tanks and natural fermenting agents – plus a mixture of sugar dissolved in wine – are then added. The wine is then bottled and sealed. The conversion of sugar into alcohol and carbonic acid ensures the second fermentation and the imprisoned gas produces the bubble or sparkle when the cork is drawn.

The second fermentation, which transforms a still wine into a sparkling one, must be very slow. During this time the bottles are shaken gently from time to time. A sediment forms gradually on the sides of the bottles, although the wine itself is clear by the end of the fermentation. The act of disposing of this sediment is called *remuage*. The bottles are then placed necks downwards; on racks at an angle of forty-five degrees. Then each day highly skilled workers give the bottles a sharp twist, a slight shake and a turn of forty-five degrees to left or right. A real expert can handle up to thirty thousand bottles a day. After eight to twelve weeks sediment will have collected in the neck of the bottle, which has been tilted gradually until, by this time, it is vertical.

The removal of this sediment is called the *dégorgement*, which must be done without losing the sparkle and with a minimal loss of wine. The modern way is to plunge the neck of the bottle through a refrigerating tank so that ice forms enclosing the sediment against the cork. This, when drawn, ejects the ice and the sediment. The small amount of wine lost is then replaced by more wine of the same *cuvée* and by a small quantity of liqueur made from old Champagne of the best quality and also by the addition of pure cane sugar. The proportion of sugar is governed by the type of wine required. This varies from *Brut* (the driest), *Sec* (slightly less dry), *Demi-Sec* (only semi-sweet) to *Doux* (sweet).

Finally, very tough corks of the finest quality are fitted, for only by the most stringent selection can a total seal be achieved which ensures that no gas whatever can escape. When affixed, each cork is secured in position by a small wire cage.

Now perhaps it will make sense to you as to why Champagne is so costly to buy.

THE LOIRE

In general the wines of the Loire area of France are white, but there are two districts which produce excellent red ones: Bourgueil on the north bank of the river Loire and Chinon on the south bank; the latter stretches down to and across the river Vienne. As with other lesser-known wines, and if you are to appreciate them to the full, you must judge them on their own qualities and characteristics and not make invidious comparisons between either of them and the red wines of Bordeaux and Burgundy.

These *Touraine* red wines are made from fully ripe black grapes and they are generally stalked (*égrappés*) when picked and before pressing. The stalks are removed by a machine called an *égrenoir* which is a funnel-shaped rotating barrel with a wooden or wicker frame, a screen and a grater. This latter stirs up the bunch of grapes with a long wooden paddle, to separate fruit from stalks. The 'must' is then left in an open wooden or cement vat to ferment for about eighteen hours. By this time most of the dust and dirt has been disposed of so that the clear wine can then be drawn off into casks where it completes its fermentation slowly – usually in about three weeks. Normally these wines are ready for the bottling process in two years, but in fact are seldom bottled until the third year after their harvesting.

It would be fair to divide the wines of these two districts into the males and females, although they are of practically the same alcoholic strength. Those of Chinon are female, being more delicate and of greater elegance than power. They have a distinct bouquet which is markedly evocative of violets. The best growths are *Les Clozeaux, La Rochelle, Rochette, Saint-Jean, Sainte-Louans* and *La Vauzelle*.

The *Bourgueils* are much more male in character, altogether bigger and stronger. Their scent is much more likely to remind you of raspberries. They are better known than the *Chinon* wines because there is a much greater production. Some of the best known are *Le Clos de la Turellière, Le Clos de la Gardiére, Le Clos de la Chevalerie, Le Clos du Fondis,* all of which come from in and around Saint-Nicholas-de-Bourgueil. From Bourgueil itself come *Le Grand Clos, Le Clos des Perrières, Le Clos de l'Abbaye* and *Le Clos de la Salpetrerie*. It is almost superfluous to remind you that, as in the case of all but the great travellers, such as *Champagne, Claret* and *Burgundy*, all the wines of these two regions are at their best when drunk *in situ*. There are many instances of wines which flatly refuse to budge from their homes. One of the most notable examples of these is *Château Chalon*, which is from France's Jura. This is a delicate and exquisite apricot-coloured wine when drunk *in situ*, but even if it has only travelled as far as Paris it then tastes like a sour, vinegary Vermouth.

Apart from the red wines of Chinon and Bourgueil the Loire is noted, principally, for its white wines, many of which are very good indeed, but it would be unreasonable to lay claim for them that they are capable of achieving greatness. It is an interesting fact too that in the Loire the vintage dates are of less account than in many other wine-producing areas. This is because it is exceptional for there to be a bad year and year by year the wines are consistent. There are some which age fairly well, but for once you can accept that it is a sound generalization to claim that in the main they are at their best when drunk fresh and young.

Now we must move across the district from west to east, following the river Loire to find the first important wine district, Nièvre, where some first-rate, dry, white wines exist around the little town of Pouilly-sur-Loire. Easily the best of these is *Pouilly-Fumé*, or, as it is sometimes called, *Blanc Fumé de Pouilly*. Now this can prove a very muddling business, as under either name this wine has nothing to do with the white Burgundy called *Pouilly-Fuissé*.

Pouilly-Fumé is admired and enjoyed for its very distinctive smoky, flinty flavour and you can expect it to have a bottle life of several years. If I were asked to single out any particular wine of this group I would recommend to you *Château de Nozet* which will also stay the course in bottle for quite a number of years. Conversely the ordinary *Pouilly-sur-Loire* wines, which are a great deal lighter, are only really enjoyable when they are young and you must also remember when tasting them that you will not find the smoky, flinty flavour I spoke of earlier, or as it is sometimes called, the 'gunflint' flavour and, indeed, aroma. These wines of the Pouilly district are all to be found on the north bank of the river.

Now let us cross to the south bank for the wines of Sancerre. These are very similar in character but I think that most tasters would agree that they are markedly lighter. Again if I were asked to make a single choice I would recommend *Château de Sancerre* as being outstanding in the area.

If you move on a little, travelling away from the river in a south-westerly direction, you will, I hope, discover, when exploring here, the little town of Quincy. Here you will find a white wine of the same name, and if you are making a vinous expedition then note that this is a typical example of a light white wine which is well worth ferreting out and drinking *in situ*, but is not of sufficient depth of character to stand long journeys. Just drink once, leave the rest behind and bring back the memory unimpaired.

Moving on again, going due west, we enter the Touraine and find ourselves among the white wines of Vouvray. Vouvray is situated on the north bank of the Loire and is famous for both still and sparkling table wines. The latter are made by the 'Champagne' method. The grapes are gathered before they are fully ripe and it is this which produces both dryish and semi-dry white wines hereabouts. I cannot honestly describe the still or natural wines as being fully dry or fully sweet. Moreover, I must admit they are normally only worth drinking in years of exceptional vine harvest. When the harvest is obviously outstanding the grower waits until the grapes are really mature and then selects the best of the best. The resultant wines made from this selection are sweet and fragrant, still retaining a characteristic freshness and yet very delicate. Vouvray also has its own wine order, *La Confrérie de la Chantepleure*, which title is derived from the name for a wine barrel's spigot (a small plug for stopping a vent hole in a cask) which is said to sing (*chante*) as the barrel is broached and thereafter to weep (*pleure*). Like all these wine orders, *Confrérie* has tremendous meetings and cele- brations. Its members dress themselves in robes of local choice and design. Indeed, you will observe throughout all France the suppres- sed longing for the pomp and ceremony of the old monarchical days which is inherent in every Frenchman's nature expressed in this fashion. To console themselves for the absence of royal ceremony and dress, almost every branch of art, music, literature and wine growing has its 'orders', its medals and its grand and impressive robes.

Let us move now to the town of Montlouis which faces Vouvray and produces a similar type of wine which is a little less distinguished and certainly lighter in character. Heading down the river once again, we come to Anjou which is responsible for that good and well-known rosé wine, but certainly much finer are the clean- tasting, slightly sweet, sparkling or dry still wines of Saumur, just south of Anjou. You will also discover here some very sound dessert wines in that particular area called Côteaux du Layon. Their main claim to distinction is a light wine called *Quarts de Chaume*. Then nearest to the mouth of the river you will come to the district of Muscadet, producing wines of that name which are universally known, pale yellow in colour, light and dry and perfectly suited to being drunk young in company with shellfish of all descriptions.

On the edge of the Loire region in the Loir-et-Cher Département I would like to draw your attention to a rosé wine called *Montri- chard* from the village of that name, hard by that most wonderful of *châteaux*, Chenonceaux. This is a wine that is described as medium sweet and when I heard the description I was very uncertain as to what the taste would be like. I discovered that, to my palate, the description was very misleading. I submit it would be much better described as medium dry. Incidentally the name Montrichard is like the name Montrachet in pronunciation, you drop the 't' in both and say 'Monrichard', as indeed you say 'Monrachet'.

THE SAVOIE AND THE JURA

There are a great number of French wines which are almost unknown in England for that same old but very valid reason that they are such bad travellers. Two typical examples are the wines of the Savoie and Jura. It is true to say that neither of these regions produces any great vintage wines, but it would be equally true to say that both have much which is worth drinking and that the areas justify a visit if only to taste their whites, reds and rosés. The two districts are situated to the east of the Côte de Beaune and they run up to the Swiss border, so, as my wife and I have done on several occasions, when visiting Switzerland you can plan, without a great detour, to sample these wines as you head towards the Swiss border.

The Savoie vineyards have produced wine since the earliest Roman times and it is on record that the great Roman gourmet Lucullus, from whom so many dishes have taken their name, served these wines at his table. They are divided into three district regions, firstly the north from Evian to Annermasse by the shores of the lake of the same name; this also takes in the great river Arve to Bonneville and runs along the Swiss border to St Julien-en-Genevois. There we find light semi-sparkling wines which have a fine aroma of almonds. Among them I would recommend to you for sampling the *Côteaux-de-Crépy* and *Petit Crépy*. This flavour is also marked in the dry white wines of Ripaille-Marin and Marignan.

The second area is in the centre, on the left bank of the Rhône and around Lac Bourget. From here we get much fuller-bodied and fruitier wines, such as *Seyssel, Marestel, Monthoux* and *Frangy*. From Seyssel you can also obtain a sparkling white wine.

The third region is in the South, around Chambéry along the right bank of the river Isère taking in the Arch valley. Here you will find more white wines, naming themselves after the regions from which they originate. They include *St-Jean-de-la-Porte, Monterminod, Asymes, Chignin, Cruet* and in addition one or two light rosés and reds which you might care to sample. Chambéry also produces one of the finest of all the Vermouths. This is not always easy to find in England, but it is possible and again is well worth a persistent quest.

The Jura vineyards extend from St Amour in the south to Salin in the north. They too produce a number of purely local wines, plus three which are widely known. First then the Côtes-du-Jura, fruity, dry, white wines and some deceptively heady red wines; both of these are rather acid when drunk extremely young, so should be given time to mature. You will also find among the Vins d'Arbois some much finer reds and rosés. These build up in this chronicle to that greatest and most unusual *Château-Chalon*, sometimes called a *Vin Jaune* because it is of a markedly amber colour. It is produced by normal vinification until the spring of the second year, then it is put into barrels which are already impregnated with earlier vintages. Here it is left quite undisturbed for six years and only after this very long period is it put into bottle. It is an experience to drink on the spot, but a pitfall for the unwary who have drunk it in its own ground; for to pick it out on some unselective wine list in an alien area is a sin. We made this cardinal error ourselves once having found it so delicious in the Jura and bitterly regretted a silly waste of money and a horrid experience for our palates. This area also has the distinction of making a sparkling dessert wine by the champagne method which is called *Vin de Paille* or Straw Wine. This is made from grapes gathered in late autumn. They are stored on straw until the following February and only then are submitted to the routine pressing procedures after which the wine is stored in small oak casks. Incidentally, there is an historic link here with the great Louis Pasteur who was born in Arbois. He actually owned a vineyard there and conducted all his early work on fermentation in his own village.

PROVENCE

The wines of Provence, like the climate, are light and sunny; they are not serious but are the natural produce of an area where the warmth and sunlight provoke thirst, which for any Frenchman is always agreeably quenched by a glass of well-cooled, light wine.

My wife and I have spent a fairly high proportion of our time in this part of France, she from when she was a very small girl and I from the first time I went to France as a schoolboy, and never at any time have we enjoyed drinking great wines there. It is almost inevitable that such wines have been cellared for some time and the frightening thing is that right through the summer the temperature is such that the great wines mature far too quickly and suffer as a result. Of course, they will be far too heavy during the summer months and I fear you will be bitterly disappointed with them at any time of year.

There is a fair amount of red wine made in Provence; in my opinion it is really not worth considering as it does not compare in quality or taste with the wines of the other red-wine-growing areas of this great wine-producing country, nor indeed do any of them stand comparison with even simple red wines from other European countries.

The wine growers of Provence produce a large quantity of white and rosé wines. These, although seemingly light and fruity, have a pretty high alcoholic content and are distinctly heady. Or to put it another way, they are as gay and exhilarating as one of the many flower festivals which crop up so frequently throughout the region.

In recent years great efforts have been made to control the quality of these wines and now the very best come under the heading 'Appellation Contrôlée'. This simply signifies wines of good quality produced from specific types of grapes, in French the initials 'V.D.Q.S.' designate wines in limited production and of superior quality and mean *Vins délimités de qualité supérieure*.

Without doubt the best of the Provençal wines – white, rosé and red – come from the region of Bellet, a smallish vineyard area nestling in the hills behind Nice. They are made in very limited quantity and are only supplied to the very best restaurants. Others which are both well-known and of sound reputation include *Château de Ste-Roseline, Château de Selle, Domaines Ott, Château de Minuty, Domaine de St-Martin* and *Pradel*.

Around Marseilles there is a local wine called *Cassis* which takes its name from the village of Cassis. This is offered practically as a matter of course with *Bouillabaisse* – that extraordinary fish soup meal which is a pungent and well-nigh overwhelming agglomeration of fourteen different Mediterranean fish. Be careful when ordering *Cassis* or you may be given an aperitif made up of a glass of white wine with a spoonful of blackcurrant concoction stirred into it. *Cassis* is also the name of a blackcurrant syrup made in Burgundy and sold all over France. So, to be sure of what you will receive ask for the *Vin Blanc de Cassis* NOT a 'Vin-Blanc Cassis'.

If you are travelling to the South of France for your holiday try to make a slight detour to the north or south of the Route Nationale. Thus you may arrive at your destination via the 'wine route' which is very clearly defined. Then you can visit the cellars and taste the wines *in situ*. After which, of course, you can make, as always, your own choice.

LANGUEDOC AND ROUSSILLON

This is a flourishing area of vast wine production, about fifteen per cent of which comprises carefully prepared wines of very reasonable quality. The remaining eighty-five per cent is of ordinary wines for immediate everyday drinking.

The Département de Herault gives us a number of authenticated (V.D.Q.S.) wines such as *Vesargues, Mejanelle, Pic Saint-Loup, Cabrières, Côteaux-du-Languedoc,* and some aromatic muscat wines like *Clairette du Languedoc* and *Mireval.* In the small village of Murviel, which lurks in the foothills just backing up from the sea, we can encounter an excellent wine of the same name. It is in fact a very full-bodied dry rosé. The local nickname for it is 'Vin d'un Nuit' (Wine of one night). It is so called because the grape skins are only allowed to ferment with the juices for a few hours.

The Gard Département boasts the good rosés of *Tavel, Chusclan* and *Lirac*; these I think you will find are very fruity and comparable with the best of any other region. Also look out for a fruity, dry white wine called *Beaucaire* from the town of Beaulave.

The Aude Département has the second largest production of wines of any French department; there the wines of quality are *Corbières, Minervois,* and *Blanquette de Limoux,* which last is a sparkling white wine. Most of the *Corbières* are strong reds which improve with age. The vineyards grow right up to the walls of the old fortified town of Carcassonne and are the source of a lusty red wine also called *Carcassonne*. This one is ideal to drink with the famous regional speciality *Le Cassoulet de Castelnaudary*; strictly a winter dish, I must emphasize. Two other recommended wines from this area are *Château de Vedrilhan*, a red wine from Narbonne and *Château des Cheminières*, a rather heady, very dry white. Then from Frontignan there is a wine which is slightly fortified and made from Muscat grapes.

In the Roussillon district we find ourselves among natural sweet wines; the sweet white, red and rosé wines of *Banyuls* are unsweetened and unfortified, and the sweetness is caused by their being from grapes which are so rich and ripe that they retain some unfermented sugar even after fermentation has ceased.

The wines of Maury will be found to be a dark red or brick colour. With age they develop special taste which is termed 'Rancio'. Finally there is Rivesalte producing a golden-tinted white wine which acquires a burnt topaz colour in maturity.

It is of some interest that the Spanish influence intrudes across the border in this part of the world. The Catalan drinks his wine from a *porron*, a carafe made of glass with a long spout, which is held at arm's length and then tipped up to produce a fine jet which must, of course, be aimed at the mouth. It requires quite a bit of practice to master this art and the inexperienced may well take the correct aim and yet receive a squirt in the eye.

THE WINES OF GERMANY

Wine making in Germany goes back to ancient times. There is, for example, ample evidence that it existed in the thirteenth century and it is more than probable that it was being made in some form even before the Romans invaded the north. It had a somewhat chequered career, was almost abolished in the third century A.D., then expanded again with the spread of Christianity; many of the better known vineyards were planted around the monasteries which were the earliest centres of good living. The Thirty Years War and similar engagements were responsible for further recessions and it was not until the middle of the eighteenth century that wine production really became important once again.

In early times there was a generic name for most German wines, 'Rhenish', as it was referred to by William Shakespeare. The English name of 'Hock' probably derives from the Hockheim district and eventually became a general name for all Rhine wines. In the early part of the nineteenth century the Germans began naming their wines after the various villages adjacent to their vineyards. In fact, today, German wine labels are about the most difficult in the world to understand. The first name on the label is usually that of the town or village and, like the French generics, is all that will appear on those of the cheaper wines. With the better wines, the town name is followed by that of a specific vineyard such as *Rüdesheimer Schlossberg*. Then quite frequently another word appears – the name of the type of grape. Just to add to the confusion other definitions are included such as the following:

Spätlese means the picking of selected bunches of grapes with no added sugar.

Beeren-Auslese means that the grapes are individually picked as they ripen.

Trockenbeeren-Auslese means the picking of selected grapes which have been allowed to remain on the vine until they are shrivelled and raisin-like.

Goldbeerenauslese is a synonym for the above.

Kellerabzug or *Originalabzug*: both these names signify bottled on the estate (like the French *château* bottled).

Wachstum is followed by name and means the growth of a . . .

Kabinett should mean 'this wine is superlative, fit for the owner's sideboard or cabinet'.

If you can manage to learn all these terms you will be able to practise more than a spot of one-upmanship upon your friends.

The German wine-producing areas are the most northerly in the world and this makes the workers' life and work even more arduous than the more southerly countries. They have to contend with much more severe conditions and a really hard winter can destroy great areas of vineyards. There are late frosts too, right into May, which can cause tremendous damage, so protective measures must be taken, the most common being the building of smoke-screens or fires. In some years there is poor sunshine which causes late ripening of the grapes, so it often happens that the harvesting does not begin until November with the increased likelihood of rain, frost, and perhaps even snow, with which to contend. In order to attain more body and quality the harvest is, even so, left for as long as possible to ensure ripening.

There are very rigid methods for the harvesting and the ancient rules evolved long ago still pertain, the only difference being that, whereas in feudal times the seigneurs decided everything, the dates for commencing harvesting are now decided by Commissions composed of the leading growers. They are very particular and even when the harvesting has started the growers are not allowed to gather their grapes when they please. In order to prevent the picking of grapes which are wet with dew or rain they receive extensive meteorological reports and using this information the local church bells are rung to denote the start and finish of picking time. If during the day conditions change for the worse the church bells are

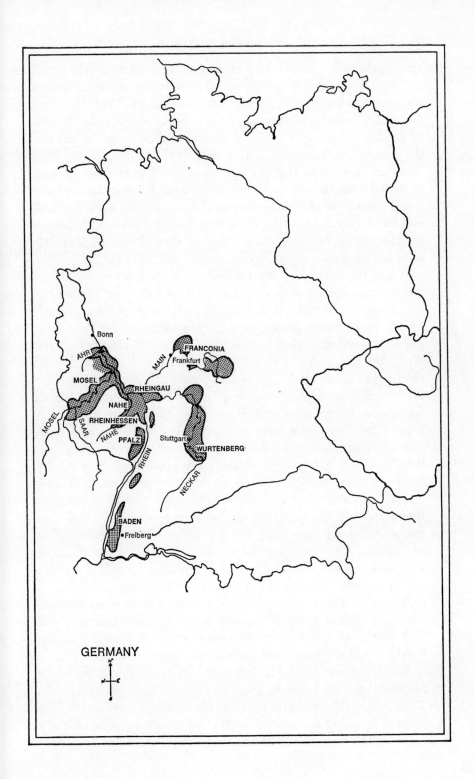

AHR

Bonn

MOSEL

FRANCONIA

MAIN

Frankfurt

RHEINGAU

MOSEL

SAAR

NAHE

RHEINHESSEN

NAHE

PFALZ

Stuttgart

WURTENBERG

RHEIN

NECKAR

BADEN

Freiberg

GERMANY

rung again to denote that all picking must cease at once. The actual picking of the grapes is performed mostly by women, with a foreman in charge of every eight to ten females. With the usual German thoroughness these pickers are encouraged to sing, the idea being that it is extremely difficult to sing and eat grapes at one and the same time. Scissors are, as a rule, used and the baskets have divisions in them so that the riper bunches of grapes can be kept separated from the rest; any diseased or damaged ones are automatically thrown out. In years when conditions are good a vineyard will be picked over twice. After the first picking the best and healthiest bunches are left to ripen further; they are then picked at a later date so that a small quantity of very fine wine can be made from them.

Unlike the old days, when the bulk of the production was of red wine, nowadays there is very little red and the vast majority is white wine. Therefore it is essential that the grapes are pressed, mostly by hydraulic presses, *on the day of picking*, as the juice must not be allowed to begin fermentation while still in contact with the pips, skin and stalks. The degree of acidity and density is very carefully noted, since it enables the grower to estimate the quality of the new wine with reasonable accuracy. Fermentation continues for several weeks, after which the wine has its first racking, in January for the lower-quality wines, in February for the finer ones. The wines are then rested, to allow them to clear, so that they may then be tasted. Six or eight weeks later, a second racking usually takes place and sometimes even further ones later on. It is now possible to bottle lighter wines fairly early, thanks to modern fining and filtering processes and so they retain their youth and freshness. On the other hand, the finer wines are never hurried, but are allowed far more time for development. They are therefore very seldom bottled until the second year after harvest, the lower qualities being bottled within the year of harvesting.

From all this you will be able to appreciate why so many German wines are expensive, but if you stick to the generic names you will find plenty of good palatable wines with the typical German fruitiness and fragrance without vast expenditure on your part.

Another reason for the higher costs incurred is that being so far north every effort has to be made to catch as much sun as possible. By experience the growers have found that this is most successfully ensured by siting the vineyards on steep slopes, but this naturally increases the costs of cultivation, as all the work must be carried out by hand and all manure, soil and spraying material be man-handled up the slopes. After planting, the ground must be regularly and thoroughly hoed. There again it is very seldom possible to employ either machines or horses.

The method of training the vines differs between the Rhine and the Moselle. In the former, the vines are kept fairly close to the ground; in many cases only one branch is retained, trained along a wire sited about three feet from the ground. In the Moselle the vines are grown on poles about four feet apart and six to seven feet high; all the old wood is cut away, only two or three of the best branches being retained. These are then bent outwards and downwards into a loop and tied securely into position.

Although wines are made in several other parts of Germany, and are really only fit for local consumption, do remember that, with the exception of the wines of Franconia, the good wines all come from either the Rhine or the Moselle.

The Rhineland has four main wine-growing districts: the 'Rheingau', the 'Palatinate', or 'Pfalz', the 'Rheinhessen' and the 'Nahe Valley'.

The 'Rheingau' is generally considered as the home of Germany's finest wines. They are well balanced, delicate and mellow. The area lies between Hochheim, the most easterly point, and Assmannshausen on a part of the Rhine which flows from east to west. Here you will find many very famous names such as *Rauenthal, Erbach, Hallgarten, Schloss Vollrads, Johannisberg* and *Rudesheim*, and, of course, many more. Incidentally, the village of Hallgarten produced a wonderful family who took their name from the village and S. F. (Fritz) Hallgarten is probably the leading authority on German wines in England. I have already said that Germany does not produce great red wines, but although theirs can in no way compare with French reds, the Red Hocks of Assmannshausen are better than most and in a good year are soft and delicate.

The 'Palatinate' is further south on the left bank of the Rhine, the vineyards being some twelve miles from the river. They produce, in general, a quantity of cheaper, ordinary wines. There are, however, some names that are well known too, like *Deidesheim, Duerkheim* and *Wachenheim* and these give us a fuller-bodied, fruitier wine than that of the 'Rheingau', but in general without the finesse or lasting quality.

The 'Rheinhessen' covers a very large area from Worms to

C

Bingen and produces great quantities of medium-class, robust wines, but when the climatic conditions are favourable, such places as *Oppenheim, Nierstein* and *Bodenheim* make very fine-quality wines. The name which is the most familiar of any German wine is *Liebfraumilch*, which originated in this area from a number of small vineyards enclosed by the walls of the *Liebfrauenstift* in Worms. This was gradually extended until the name became generic for a reasonable, soft wine of fair quality. Unfortunately it has been exploited shamelessly and while a genuine *Liebfraumilch* is an excellent, medium-dry wine you can be foisted off with some very bad stuff; so make sure you buy from a reliable source.

The 'Nahe Valley' produces wines of great elegance which are lighter than most Rhine wines and begin to approach those of the Moselle. The best of all comes from Schloss Bockelheim – it is very pale, highly scented, fresh and fruity. After it the next best are the wines of Niederhausen and Kreuznach.

The German portion of the Moselle starts at the Swiss border and continues until it joins the Rhine at Koblenz. As a generalization it may be said that the Moselle wines are lighter and drier than the Rhine wines, but they have great character and are really delightful both as aperitifs and table wines. The river winds and twists so much that it covers over forty miles, although as the crow flies the distance is only eighteen. It is obvious from this fact that the wines vary tremendously. The ground rises steeply from the river to seven or eight hundred feet in places and the steeper the slope the better the wine, especially where the vineyards face south or south-west. The first village of consequence is Klusserath and the wine is called *Bruderschaft*; it is light and very reasonable.

We next come to Trittenheim, with its light, delicate and fresh wines. The first world-wide-known name hereabouts is *Piesport* and the *Piesporter Goldtropfchen*, rounded and slightly sweet, has a wonderful fragrance.

Now comes the greatest vineyard of the Moselle, Bernkastel. The town is a magnificently medieval one with its timbered buildings, narrow alleys and the wonderful Renaissance Town Hall built in 1608. Overlooking it is the very steep slope on which the vineyards are sited; these produce the best of the Bernkastel wines, *Bernkasteler Doktor*. The Bernkastel wines are drier than the average Moselles and have a slightly flinty flavour while preserving the fruity fragrance which is so typical of this part of the world. The *Doktor* vineyard is very small, so it is understandable that the wines are so highly priced.

A few miles from here is Wehlen and nowadays its wines are more prized and higher priced than the *Doktor*. The *Wehlener Sonnenuhr* (sun-dial) is without question my favourite Moselle wine; it is so rich and full of flavour, yet somehow fresh and delicate! An outstanding sight here is the giant sun-dial sculptured out of an overhanging cliff in the face of the vineyard. When you are feeling flush give yourself a memorable experience and try your best to remember this great wine.

Adjacent is another village called Zeltingen which also produces a most beautiful wine usually named *Zeltinger Sonnenuhr*, or in the case of one vineyard *Wehlener-Zeltinger Sonnenuhr*.

There are so many good vineyards in the Moselle which will provide you with good, sound wines and I have just singled out the most notable for your attention.

In Germany there is a tremendous industry in sparkling wine, of which the Germans themselves consume an immense quantity; this type is known under the generic name *Sekt* and is usually dry. Some of the best costs almost as much as Champagne, but there is a lot made that is medium priced and quite palatable for those who cannot afford the real thing. Be careful, however, in buying this *Sekt* because the cheapest is made from wine brought in by tanker from Italy, Spain and even Africa, and sold with the addition of a small quantity of German wine to make sure that the original character is not noticed. You should be safe if you go to a reliable merchant and ask him for a sparkling Moselle.

No chapter on German wines would be complete without the mention of an oddity that is special to that country. *Eiswein* (ice-wine) is only made in years with a hard winter and is produced from grapes that are gathered, often in the snow, very early in the morning when the frost has frozen the juice in them; they must be pressed while they are still frozen. This is not for us because the cost is prohibitive.

There is one sure way for the beginner to distinguish between the Rhine and the Moselle wines. The Rhine ones are in a brown bottle while those of the Moselle are in a green bottle. So no one need ever disclose their lack of knowledge, at least in this respect.

THE WINES OF ITALY

Italy is one of the oldest wine producers in the world; it is also the biggest wine producer in the world, but until very recently the quality of these wines has never been comparable with those of France, or indeed Germany. The great trouble in the past was that very little attention seemed to be given to the cultivation and production except to ensure vast quantities of table wine which had to be drunk almost immediately. Great unevenness of quality resulted; you might drink a bottle of a red or white and find it extremely good, order a case or two, only to discover, on tasting, that the next bottle of the same wine was entirely different and maybe positively undrinkable.

Fairly recently leading Italian wine shippers formed an organization which won the wholehearted support of the Italian Government. In character it somewhat resembled the French *Appeation Contrôlée*. It took the name *Denominazione di Origine Controllata*, normally abbreviated to D.O.C. This is beginning to gain ascendancy all over the country, not least in the main wine-growing areas; as in France, it limits the area entitled to bear the name of any given wine. It also regulates the amount of wine which can be produced per acre and states the types of grape to be employed. Experts travel around incessantly conducting tasting-tests and making certain that regulations for the production are obeyed. The resultant wines are, therefore, much more even. Thus my only advice on this matter is to ensure you buy D.O.C. approved wines.

Taken as a whole, Italy does not at the moment export much of her best wine – only wines of medium quality. Many wine lovers prefer Italian red wines to their white ones, but I beg leave to disagree and incline very strongly towards the dry whites, when they can be drunk young and fresh.

In Italy the vines are trained up trellises and are not ground bushes. My gastronomic 'Papa', the late André L. Simon, accounts for the acidity of Italian wines by the difficulty the grapes have in ripening even in a hot climate if they are grown at any distance from the ground. The vineyards stretch from the Swiss border right down to Sicily. White wines are made in every part of the country but as a generalization, the good red wines are all made in Tuscany and to the north of this region. At present Italian wines do not have a long life and do not mature appreciably in bottle. The ordinary wines should be left about three years before drinking and the better ones are at their best when about five years old.

So now let us consider the wines, region by region, starting in the north and working down south to Sicily.

Piedmont has a variety of good-quality wines, and although red wines predominate there are a number of white to be found, both dry and sweet in character. There is one outstanding red, *Barolo*, known as the 'king of Italian wines' or the 'wine of kings' because in the nineteenth century it was the favourite of the kings of the house of Savoy. It comes from the area in the hills around Alba, and is strong, with a rich bouquet, but when young is very sharp. It requires a time to mature, so is protected by law which stipulates it must be kept in oak barrels for at least three years, by which time it has turned orangy red in colour and, while still remaining dry, has lost its initial sharpness. Another red wine which is similar to *Barolo* comes from nearby; it is called *Barbaresco*. Also kept in oak, it is nevertheless much faster in maturing.

Lesser-known ones include *Sizzano, Lessona, Gattinara, Fara, Ghemme, Boca* and *Mottalciata*; all need time to mature before drinking.

From the hillsides by the Aosta Valley comes a lighter-coloured wine called *Carema*. Nearly half the total production of Piedmont is taken up by *Barbera* and a genuine mature *Barbera d'Asti* is very good drinking. Also produced in quantity is another red which can be dry or semi-dry is quicker to mature and is called *Freisa*.

A dry wine from a sweet grape is named *Dolcetto*, there is also a sparkling variety of it. Finally, from a very small area comes what many people think is the best of the Piedmont wines – *Grignolino*.

The best of the white wines are the *Cortese*, which indicates a straw-coloured, light, dry wine, and *Erbaluce di Caluso*, which is also dry. Before we leave Piedmont I must mention a wine that has acquired a world-wide reputation among sparkling wines – *Asti Spumante*. I hasten to add that this is not among my personal selection – ever! There is also a red sparkling wine which carries the scent of roses called *Brachetto*.

Next we come to the province of Lombardy which is divided into three main areas. First, along the western side of Lake Garda, we find rosé and red wines, the rosés being on the sweet side but the reds being smoother, but still a little bitter. There is too *Lugana* of a greeny straw colour and quite dry, plus the products of a small vineyard making red, white and rosé under the name *Pusterla*.

Next we find the Oltrepo of Pavia. Hereabouts we find the dry white wines *Canneto, Clastidio* and *Frecciarossa;* all have a good bouquet. The reds are mellow, of medium alcoholic strength and are slightly acid. The best are *Monte-Napoleone, Clastidio,* and three with colourful names, *Barbacarlo* meaning 'Charles's Beard', *Sangue di Giudo* meaning 'The Blood of Judas' and *Buttafuoco* meaning 'Fire Propagator'. There are also some good aperitif wines such as the red *Canneto Dolce*.

Thus we come to the Valteline where the vineyards are planted on precipitous slopes to which the workers have to crawl to tend the vines and also gather the grapes. The wines are named from the districts such as *Grumello, Inferno, Villa, Sassella*. They are deep-coloured, full-bodied and smooth.

Now we move on to Liguria, not a great wine-growing area but notable for one unique wine the *Cinqueterre* which takes its name from five villages all famous for their vineyards and all situated on land which runs down to the sea on such steep slopes that some can only be reached by boat or by ropes and ladders from the cliffs above. It is not a sinecure to work in such Italian vineyards; it is, however, a great advantage to have the propensities of a mountain goat.

The Three Venetias area is about equal with Apulia for the quantity of wine produced. The district of Trentino gives us good-quality red and white wine, among the best being *Teroldego*, a bright red wine with a 'bouquet' of raspberries, and a lighter-coloured one called *Marzemino*. The finest whites hereabouts are *Traminer, Riesling Italico* and some of the semi-sparkling ones.

The Bolzano district produces whites like *Terlano*. This is a light,

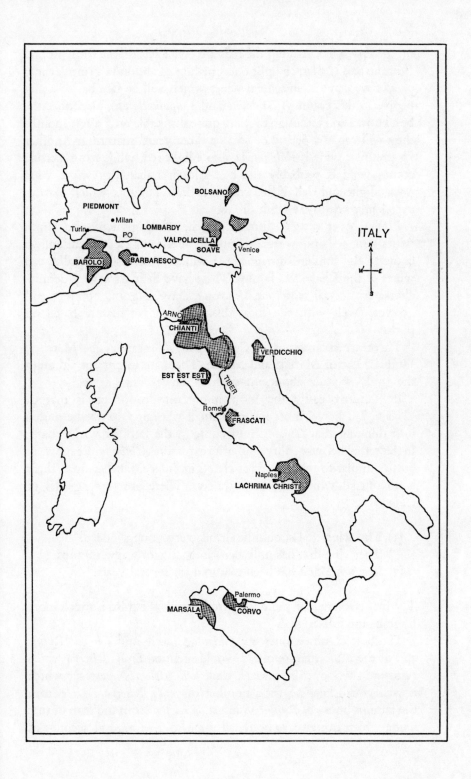

ITALY

PIEDMONT
Milan
Turin
PO
LOMBARDY
BOLSANO
VALPOLICELLA
SOAVE
Venice
BAROLO
BARBARESCO

ARNO
CHIANTI
VERDICCHIO
EST EST EST
TIBER
Rome
FRASCATI

Naples
LACHRIMA CHRISTI

Palermo
MARSALA
CORVO

dry greeny wine, Among the reds are *Santa Maddellena* from around
Bolzano and *Caldaro*, a light one smelling of almonds. From Veneto
proper we can obtain several wines which will be familiar to many
people in this country. *Bardolino* and *Valpolicella* are, of course, the
best known and although they are quite drinkable after a few months
they will repay a period of two or three years' maturing. Another
very similar wine is *Valpantena*, also a light red, while from Verona
comes what is probably the best-known Italian dry white wine
Soave, light and delightful, with a delicate bouquet which marries
excellently with many fish dishes.

Passing over several districts which, while giving quite sound
wines both red and white, do not relly merit our close attention, we
come to the Emilia Romagna area which produces the quality red
wines of the *Lambruschi* family. These have their own very definite
characteristics, all rather acid, strong, have a good bouquet and
go very well with the local dishes which are mainly based on
pork.

There are six regions in Central Italy, Tuscany, The Marches,
Umbria, Lazio, Abruzzi and Molise. These are important although
they only produce about one-sixth of the country's wine.

In Tuscany easily the most important production is that of
Chianti, but here I must record a small warning: do not be misled
into thinking that *Chianti* must come in the familiar wicker flask.
In fact the better-quality and more mature *Chiantis* are now in
bottles similar to those used for clarets in France. Furthermore, there
is no official white *Chianti* nowadays. There are three grades of
Chianti:

(1) The wine that should be drunk very young indeed.
(2) The wine that has only been in bottle for a few months.
(3) The wine that has been matured for several years.

The first two are fruity and very fresh, while the third is much more
fragrant and full-bodied.

The best classified ones are *Chianti Classico* and *Chianti Rufina*
and of the more mature ones I would mention *Brolio Riserva* which
remains in wood for five years, *Castello di Meleto*, *Nipozzano* which
is well worth keeping for a number of years, *Riserva Ducale* from
the famous house of *Ruffino*, *Stravecchio Melini* from the firm of that
name which can always be relied upon to give a good account of

itself, and finally *Villa Antinori*. This last house sells a variety of wines and in my experience all are of the highest quality.

Other Tuscan wines include *Montecarlo* which is sold both red and dry white. The nicest way to sample them is to choose an evening in the summer when the renowned midnight trotting races are on. Dine at leisure in the open air in the attractive Montecatini Spa Piazza, and sample these wines; they induce just the right mood for indulging thereafter in a gambling session at the racecourse. Nor must I omit to mention *Ugolino Bianco*, a fresh dry wine which has a slight prickle (Spritzig), *Vino Nobile di Montepulciano* which is a good red wine, if not broached when too young, *Vin Santo* which is a rich dessert wine and probably the greatest red wine of the area and *Brunello di Montalcino*, which is left in the wood for at least five years and is then kept for two years in bottle before being released.

The Marches produce two wines which merit your attention. First comes *Bianchello* a light, dry white wine in varying qualities; then I would recommend *Bianchello del Matauro* and *Verdicchio dei Castelli di Jesi*, one of the best white wines of the country. Due to its high alcoholic content, this last travels very well. Do not allow yourselves to be put off by the distinctly vulgar labels!

Undoubtedly the most favoured wine of Umbria is *Orvieto*, which was originally the *Orvieto Abboccato* (semi-sweet), this degree of sweetness being obtained by allowing the grapes to begin rotting after picking. It is not by any means a dessert wine and would appeal most to those who find the really dry wines a bit too sharp for their palates. Comparatively recently the *Secco* (dry) variety was created and this is delightful, but it does carry a very slight bitter secondary taste. There is also *Nebbiolo*, a red wine which could be described as a poor man's *Barolo*. Other red and white wines from this region are more of local interest and are not really important to us.

The Lazio area consists of two main districts, the Castelli Romani in the hills and the region around Lago Bolsena. The wines of the former district are extremely varied, but mainly white, of which the semi-sweet and the sweet are the most prolific. The dry ones are, however, steadily gaining in popularity to suit the changing tastes of the average wine lover. Easily the best known is the *Frascati*, which is a very good golden wine produced in dry, semi-sweet, and sweet variants, of which again I prefer the dry one. At night the town of this name is full of stalls selling roast suckling pig which the inhabitants consume with great chunks of bread, and wash down with their local *Frascati* wine.

In the Lago Bolsena region we find, first and foremost, the rather delightful light white wine again produced in dry, semi-sweet and sweet versions called *Est! Est! Est!*, of which a romantic story is told. A certain bishop was on his way to Rome in A.D. 1100 for the coronation of Emperor Henry V. The bishop was a great wine lover who habitually despatched his servant one day ahead of him to report on the wine he might expect upon his arrival. If an inn satisfied this prelate, he chalked on the door the word *Est!* If not, he wrote *Non Est!* On arrival at Montefiascone, tired and dispirited, he was given a wine which pleased him so much that he chalked – for the first time ever – the triple approval *Est! Est! Est!* The sequel to this tale is that instead of going on to Rome the wine-loving bishop stayed on in Montefiascone for the rest of his life, until he eventually drank himself into his grave.

Another familiar name is *Falernum*, which signifies a dry white wine which is rather bitter and said by many to have derived from Horace's *Falernian*.

The Abruzzi and Molise areas form a narrow coastal strip which is backed by mountains. The majority of the grape production is only fit for making lower-quality sparkling wines, or else it is simply used for blending. There is a small amount of rather ordinary red, white and rosé wine, but this is drunk locally and goes quite well with the dishes of the region.

We now come to the southern part of the country where the first area is Campania (around Naples), famous for *Lacrima Christi*, a name which must be familiar to most people. Just be cautious as to what you buy under this name, for it has become rather like *Lieb-fraumilch*. In effect the genuine wine is a very good dry, fruity white, which goes well with fish dishes, but make sure you obtain it from a reliable wine merchant or you may find yourself landed with something of very inferior quality under the same name. Also from this region comes red and white *Falerno*, not to be con-fused with the *Falernum* mentioned earlier. This is the better-known wine and it too claims descent from Horace, probably with more justification.

From the islands of Capri and Ischia come red and white wines of no particular significance. Of the two islands I much prefer those of Ischia, especially the dry white if drunk when it is very young. Of the other wines from Campania, those of *Ravello* are palatable; the rosé, however, is a bit sweeter than the average and thus rather cloying on the palate.

The three most southern areas of Italy are Apulia, the Basilicata and Calabria, where more wine is produced than in any other part of the country. However, due to the very hot, strong sun and the heavy soil, the wines are coarse and heavy. The whites are chiefly used for Vermouth; the reds are reserved for blending.

We cannot leave Italy, however, without discussing the wines of Sicily. There is a well-balanced, pale, refreshing, dry white wine to be found under the name of *Corvo Bianco*; this I submit is not adequately appreciated in Britain as yet. The *Corvo Rosso* is also a very good red wine, well worthy of your attention.

Last but by no means least we find *Marsala*, a rich fortified wine which has unfortunately fallen out of favour with the British in recent years. Today it is generally considered as a cooking wine *tout court*! This is regrettable. During both the Regency and Victorian periods it was regarded as a great rival to Madeira; it had, and indeed still has, the added advantage of being lower in price. *Marsala* is made by adding a small quantity of brandy and a larger quantity of sweet wine to the bulk base of dry wine. After this young grape juice is incorporated *before it has fermented*. It is first heated very gradually until it becomes sweet, syrupy, thick and brown and then is added to the rest. Finally, *Marsala* is rested in the wood for anything from six months to five years.

If you are wondering at the total omission of Italian Vermouth, please do so no longer. You will find it has a chapter to itself (p. 162).

THE WINES OF SPAIN

The average Englishman immediately thinks of Sherry when Spanish wines are mooted; alas, this range of fine, fortified wines is only a very small part of today's story. We sometimes overlook the fact that Spain produces a very large quantity of table wine from vineyards which are flourishing in many parts of the country. In point of fact it is probable that vine cultivation in Spain goes as far back as the time when the Phoenicians traded with the Spaniards. It is certainly true that the Romans introduced serious wine growing during the hey-day of their Empire.

One of the most interesting features of viniculture in Spain is that it is carried on in conjunction with olive culture, so we find that in some instances olive groves and vineyards are inextricably blended one with the other.

There is one outstanding region, the Rioja, situated in the north and comprising parts of Burgos, Alava and Navarre and all Logrono.

The next great error – one which is still committed all too frequently – is the making of invidious comparisons between Spanish wines and those of Bordeaux or Burgundy. Spanish wines, like those of other less superb wine-growing countries, should be judged on their own merit as wines which have a distinctiveness of flavour and bouquet which is all their own. This judgement is not encouraged by the Spaniards themselves, who so often label their wines 'Chablis', 'Sauternes', 'Claret' or 'Burgundy', which greatly misleads tasters.

It is probable that the main reason for the better quality of *Rioja* wine stemmed from the influx of French *Vignernons* (wine growers) who moved into the area when the great phylloxera scourge practically wiped out their own vineyards in the late nineteenth century. These men brought the great French techniques to Spain.

The region gives us a very wide choice of wines, all differing in taste, bouquet and strength due to the great number of types which are produced in various areas.

A great deal of attention is given to the ageing of the wines which must be matured for a minimum of two years of which one year must be in oak casks. The first stage in Bordeaux casks can last from two to five years. Racking then takes place during which oxidization occurs; this has the effect of stabilizing the wine. The second stage is the production. In other words, the wine is bottled and left for a varying period to mature. At the same time the aroma begins to develop. The finished wine is clear, with a strong and distinctive bouquet, and the red wine assumes a distinctly purple tinge.

The Rioja is divided into three parts: Rioja Alta to the west, from which come good wines of fairly low alcoholic strength; Rioja Baja around Logrono, yielding not quite so good a wine but one which is of higher alcoholic strength; and Rioja Alavesa, a smaller district north of the river Ebro, producing a much smoother wine.

We must always remember with these wines not to pay much attention to the year stated on any label – as the Spanish frequently employ the Solera system. This I have dealt with in depth in my chapter on Sherry, so I will merely touch upon the meaning of the word very briefly in this context. Solera means a blending of wines of various years, so that, for example, 1959 on a label may very well represent the date of the oldest wine used in the overall blend or mixture.

So that you may know what to look for when wishing to obtain a good Spanish table wine I will now set out a short list of some which I would particularly recommend.

Fine red wines called *Rioja Santiago* are available under the mark *Yago*. These come from the Bodegas Rioja Santiago and are sold in distinctive square bottles.

From the Bodegas Bilbainas you can obtain a number of red and white wines under the marks *Vina Pomal* (red), *Vina Paceta* (a dryish white) and *Brillante* (a sweet white).

From the Bodegas R. Lopez de Heredia Vina Tondonia S.A. come very dry whites called *Vina Tondonia Blanco, Vina Zaconia* (semi-dry) and *Rioja Clarete Fino* (red), which are bottled after three years 'in wood'; there is also *Vina Tondonia Tinto*, which spends six years in barrel before being bottled.

From the Bodegas Compagñia Vinicola del Norte de España I recommend *Monopole* (dry white), *Corona* (young red), *Imperial Gran Reserva* and *Vina Real Oro* for anyone preferring more mature reds.

As you will realize, there are a great number of very drinkable Spanish wines from which you can make your choice. I would only add in one more group in this Rioja region. . . .

From the Bodegas Federico Paternina, a *Banda Azul* (red), sold when about four years old, *Vina Bial* (red), sold when about ten years old, and *Gran Reserva* a much older, bigger wine altogether.

From the Bodegas Riojanas a *Monte Real*, a *Vina Albina* (reds), the latter being the drier, and also a *Medieval*, a very pale dry white.

From the Marques de Riscal, come reds under this name, and from the Marques de Murrieta three red wines *Marques de Murrieta Tinto, Marques de Murrieta Reserva Especial* and *Castillo Ygay*.

Of the other wine-growing areas by far the largest is La Mancha. This consists of four provinces, Toledo, Albaceta, Cuenca and Ciudad Real. The wines from this district provide the sound, inexpensive range which is sold throughout Spain. It goes straight from the barrel into the simple, everyday wine shops. A substantial amount of the La Mancha wines are also still sold in *Pellejos*. These are the whole skins of pigs retained in that form and therefore presenting a distinctly odd appearance. The wine keeps for very long periods in these curious containers, so look out for them in your travels, particularly in the old wine shops of Madrid. *Valdepenas* wines from Ciudad Real are the ones most frequently served from the barrel. These are drunk young, usually in the spring following the vintage, as is *Valdepenas Tinto* (red) which is much more like a rosé in colour and character. The *Valdepenas Beancho* (white) varies from very pale straw colour to the more usual rich gold.

The making process in La Mancha is fairly rudimentary. The harvest commences around the end of September. The grapes are brought in from the vineyards, weighed and then de-stalked by machinery. This process crushes them at the same time. The grapes are then fed into the *Atrojes*, which are vast containers holding up to twenty-seven or twenty-eight thousand kilos; this enormous weight soon starts the juice pouring through the slatted sides of the containers. When the juice ceases to run, the remainder is extracted by

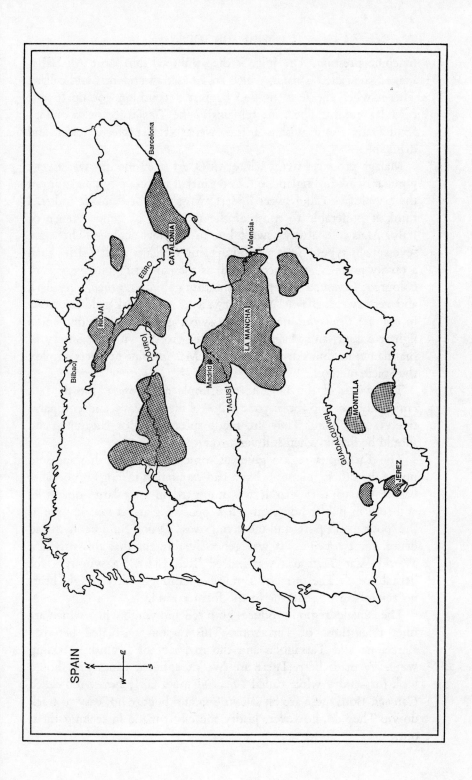

SPAIN

machine pressing. The juice is then pumped into large Ali Baba-shaped jars called *Tinajas*, which are housed in underground cellars. This is when the fermentation begins; it continues for up to one calendar month. The wine remains in the *Tinajas* for its secondary fermentation and within a few weeks it is perfectly clear and drinkable.

Malaga produces sweet white wines. At one time this was a very popular drink in England and I consider it a great pity that more of the people who like sweet dessert wines do not drink it today. I think it preferable to most of the muscatels of either France or Italy. *Malaga* is always sweet but in varying degrees. There are seven main types: *Seco*, a good aperitif which is a little drier than a tawny port; *Negro*, sweeter and, as the name suggests, very dark coloured; *Oscuro*, a rather deep chestnut colour; *Lagrima*, very dark and very sweet; *Blanco Dulce*, very sweet and a dark golden-brown in colour; *Semidulce*, not quite so sweet as the previous one and a lighter colour, and *Amontillado* (nothing to do with the Sherry of that name) medium dry. Some of the Malaga wine growers employ the Solera method.

The wines of the Levante are simple and honest, mostly red, eminently suitable for anyone who relishes a heavy and comparatively sweet wine. They are made specifically for cheapness and should be drunk when still very young.

The Tarragona region gives us some heavy sweetish wine sold under the district name. It has a bad reputation in England because before the 1914–18 war it was imported in very large quantities and sold in public houses at a few pence a glass. It was known as the 'poor man's port' and the saying was, 'Drunk for a penny, dead drunk for twopence.' It was generally thought that this pre-First World War *Tarragona* was indeed 'Red Biddy', a synonym for 'lethal brew'. The modern *Tarragona*, although fairly rough, bears no resemblance whatever to the former kind.

The Panades region produces both red and white wines which are finer than those of Tarragona. This region is situated between Barcelona and Tarragona and the majority of Spanish sparkling wines are made here. There are two exceptional wines you should look for – a dry white called *Vina Sol* and a fairly heavy red called *Coronas*. Both these are on sale in England but are not easy to track down. They do, however, justify the effort made in seeking them out.

1. Vignoble à Beaune (Côte d'Or).   *(Food from France)*

2. Harvest in 'Graves' region near Bordeaux.   *(Food from France)*

3. Picking and transporting grapes for processing. *(Cockburn, Smithes Limited)*

4. Sherry being sampled in a bodega in Jerez-de-la-Frontera. *(Harveys of Bristol)*

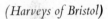

5. Cockburn's Lodge at Regua – port pipes in the cooperage. *(Cockburn, Smithes Limited)*

6. Steaming a port pipe in the cooperage at Cockburn's Lodge in Villa Nova de
    Gaia, Oporto.   *(Cockburn, Smithes Limited)*

7. Martinez – Lodges at Villa Nova de Gaia.   (*Cockburn, Smithes Limited*)

8. Vat inspection prior to filling. *(Cockburn, Smithes Limited)*

9. Sherry grapes piled to dry in the sun before pressing in the sherry vineyards near Jerez-de-la-Frontera, Spain. *(Harveys of Bristol)*

10. Sherry vintage scene in the vineyards of Jerez-de-la-Frontera. *(Harveys of Bristol)*

11.   Part of a Sherry bodega in Jerez-de-la-Frontera, where thousands of gallons lie maturing awaiting shipment all over the world.

The wines of the Castile region revolve around Valladolid, near which is the village of Rueda; this produces a golden wine with a smell and taste not unlike Sherry. Zamora and Toro contribute a dark red wine known as *Sangre de Toro* (Bull's Blood), although it must be stressed that it has nothing in common with the Hungarian wine of the same name, nor has it the slightest association with bulls.

On the coast round Sitges you will find a number of dessert wines. *Moscatel* and *Malvasia* are the two types made; both are extremely potent. *Malvasia* you will recognize from the same name wines from other countries, and the original stock was in all probability introduced from Cyprus in the Middle Ages.

The Navarre region gives us rosé wines which are very good and reds that are very deceptive because, although actually of low alcoholic strength, the red wine is a deep ruby in colour which makes it look much stronger than it in fact is.

The Aragon region yields reasonable sound wines which are usually rather sweet, both red and white. They are drunk locally when they are young and fresh.

The Estremadura area makes reasonable red and white wine, but possibly their most distinctive product is a light rosé with a higher alcoholic content than is usual. It is very ineptly called *Clarete de Guadalcanal;* It has, of course, no resemblance at all to real claret.

There are countless other Spanish table wines, most of which should be drunk *in situ*, when they taste quite agreeable, but do not attempt to bring any home or you will be deeply disappointed.

Until a few years ago the wine growers of Spain had named their white sparkling wines 'Spanish Champagne'. Then an injunction was obtained restricting them from so doing and it was established once and for all that the Champagne region of France had the sole right to the use of the name 'Champagne'.

So what many of you may have known before this official ruling as 'Spanish Champagne' is in fact a sparkling wine which fizzes in the glass. It is very confusing, even so, because it is a sparkling wine and the best is made by the Champagne method which I have described in the section on Champagne. Even so, no one with any sense would ever claim that sparkling Spanish wine is comparable to real Champagne. The Spanish sparkling wines are simply gay, light and forgotten as soon as drunk – like *vin rosés*. Because they are gay, they associate themselves with parties for those of you who like Spanish wine and are in any event unable to face the cost of

Champagne. In fact, in the party context they have a very great number of uses. You can turn them into a sparkling wine cup; use them instead of Champagne for toasts at weddings and lace them with Spanish Brandies to produce what is best described as 'Poor man's King's Peg'. Real 'King's Peg' is Champagne laced with Cognac (Brandy from Cognac) and so called because of King Edward VII's predilection for this mixture.

The main sparkling wine-producing areas of Spain are twenty miles south of Barcelona and behind the Costa Brava. The two which are generally considered to be the best are called *Codorniu* and *Perelada*. The latter is easily obtainable over here and can be bought as extra-dry vintage, or 'demi-sec' non-vintage. A very good cup can be made with one bottle of Spanish sparkling wine, 2 fl oz of Spanish Brandy, 1½ fl oz of Cointreau, 1 fl oz of Maraschino, soda water and ice. Chill the wine beforehand, pour into a jug or bowl and add the brandy, Cointreau and Maraschino, then add soda water to taste and finally stir in sixteen ice cubes.

About forty companies make sparkling wine by the Champagne method, but do make sure that any you buy has been made in this way. Unfortunately there are many firms who use a very inferior method for the sake of cheapness and make their 'sparkling wine' by fermenting it in the vat and then bottling it and selling it quickly. It is able to obtain its sparkle from the secondary fermentation which constitutes an artificial way of speeding things up. There is a third and wicked method used which consists of inducing carbonic acid gas into a still white wine.

There is a very great quantity of Brandy made in Spain and the Spaniards themselves consume a great deal of it. Some of the better ones are quite palatable if judged on their own merits, but they bear no resemblance to French Cognac and are in fact very seldom allowed to mature as they should, being drunk while still much too young and immature.

THE WINES OF PORTUGAL

It is acknowledged that the best Portuguese wines never leave their own country, but even so there are several wine connoisseurs who insist that when Portuguese wines are drunk *in situ* they equal those of many wine-making countries of far greater vinous reputation.

Having spent a month in Portugal two years ago, I beg leave to differ. Certainly there are exceptions, and among them I would unhesitatingly place some which my wife and I were privileged to drink in several private quintas. *But these are not offered for sale on the open market!*

It is an encouraging fact, however, that the authorities are trying very hard to improve standards by placing a strict form of control known as *Designação de Origen*, which is much the same as the French *Appellation Contrôlée*. In time this will have a markedly improving influence.

Probably the best known, certainly the most original, Portuguese wines are the *Vinho Verdes*, or 'green wines'. The name has absolutely nothing to do with the colour, which is generally yellow with only an occasional tinge of green. It stems from the fact that these wines are made from grapes picked while young. Furthermore, the wines themselves taste young and are drunk when young; they have, too, a slight sparkle which I describe as being more of a prickle. Their individuality stems from the fact that the Minho area in which they are grown, being in the northern part of the country, is intensely hot in summer but rainy, chilly and with brilliant green vegetation during the rest of the year. The roads and fields are almost invariably fringed by tall trees and hedges. The vines trail from bush to bush and from tree-branch to tree-branch. Sometimes they actually soar so high that ladders are required for reaching the topmost bunches at harvest time. Thus no land is ever wasted. There is room left for ground crops below, which is vital if the grapes are not to be scorched by the rising heat from the sun-baked soil.

The majority of the *Vinhos Verdes* are white wines, and only a small quantity of red wine is made. While all are an experience to drink, they are definitely an acquired taste about which no two drinkers agree. Red *Vinhos Verdes*, unlike the whites, should be left to mature for several years, though even when young they retain a distinction of character. You can find quite a number of them on sale in Britain at very reasonable prices, so you can readily discover for yourself if you are pro or anti these wines. Incidentally, they can generally be recognized on sight by the unusual shape of the bottles.

The second wine-growing area is called Dão, and is certainly the largest Portuguese wine-growing region. The majority of the wines are reds which have been blended. They are strong, fairly smooth and when matured have quite a good bouquet. They are at their best when between seven and eight years old. The white wines, which form the minority, have greater depth of character, with a hard, clean taste. They should be drunk within their first three years. In this area the weather is again wet and cold in winter and very hot in summer. This transition of climatic conditions is very rapid and the quick change from hot to cold slows up fermentation; the result is that very little 'fining' is needed. Dão is another high-growing vine district with the vines grown in small fields, either in serried rows, upon wires strung up to four feet, or else looped round tall poles when the growth reaches up to five feet.

The central Portuguese wines are found near Lisbon. They are divided into four main districts. The first is Bucelas – about fifteen miles north of Lisbon. At one time Bucelas produced a sweet white wine which was immensely popular in England, but things have changed and nowadays the white wine is much drier, having a very faint resemblance to a light Rhine wine, so is not so highly thought of here. In any event, do remember all the Bucelas wines should be drunk when young.

The second district, Carcavelos, produces a small and constantly diminishing quantity of wine. This is due to the encroachments and developments going on apace in the area of more and more

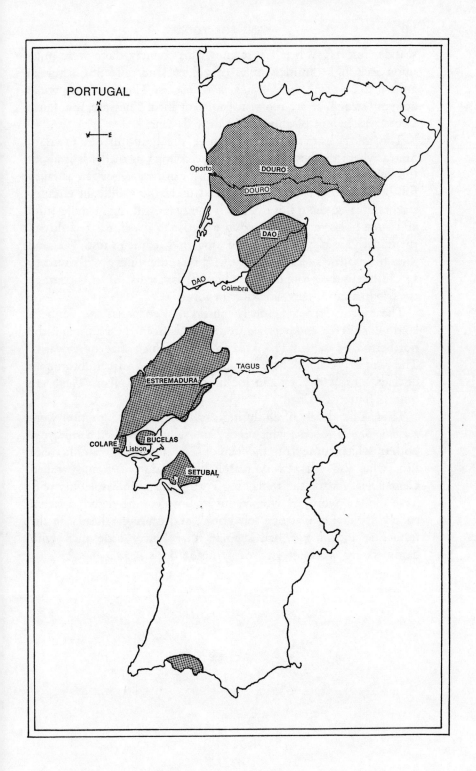

PORTUGAL

N
W—E
S

Oporto

DOURO

DOURO

DAO

DAO

Coimbra

TAGUS

ESTREMADURA

COLARE

BUCELAS

Lisbon

SETUBAL

seaside 'resorts'. When I first knew this country there were miles upon seemingly limitless miles of golden sands and not a human animal to be seen! *Autres temps, autres mœurs!* The remaining wines are very strong, so are most probably fortified. They are, too, fairly sweet with a hint of almonds in their flavour.

The third district, Colares, is near the beautiful old town of Sintra where the best red wine of the country is made. It is about the same strength as a good claret and can be categorized as fairly full-bodied. The vines are cultivated under very difficult circumstances because the soil is extremely sandy (as you might conjecture) and large holes must first be dug in order to reach, ten feet down, the underlying clay in which the roots must come to rest. The sand then fills up the holes gradually, and then the vines are allowed to spread along the ground. Thus they are layered so as to encourage the production of new, additional roots.

The fourth district, Setubal, consists of two parts: the southern land which is flat and exposed to the winds from the south, and the northern land which forms steep slopes which face northwards. The wines produced here are both white and sweet, bearing a distinct Muscat flavour and looking like liquid amber. These are quite definitely fortified.

Those I liked best of all during my last vinous exploration were a *Vinho Branco Reserva* which is dry and white, and a red *Serradayres*, both of which come from the firm of Carvalho Ribiero and Ferreira Ltd, who also sell a very reasonable Portuguese Brandy called *Constantino*. As for the remaining Portuguese Brandies, let my wife have the last word, as women invariably do. She describes them rudely as 'having a strong left hook', and causing a headache the following morning which suggests that 'thirty little men with hammers are working vigorously inside one's head'.

THE WINES OF
GREECE

As you might expect, Greece is among the oldest wine-producing
countries. Homer praised them in his *Odyssey* and the *Iliad*;
Dionysus cultivated his own vines, and the Greeks, who were great
exporters, transported their vines to both Jerez and Malaga in Spain,
to the French Rhône Valley and to Sicily. Even the Malvoisie grape
was established by them in Madeira.

The popular conception of Greek wines is that they are all bitter
with *retsina*, and it is false. To speak of a *retsina* wine is to signify
that it is flavoured with resin during the fermentation procedure;
by no means all Greek wines are so treated. The *retsina* does, however, produce a distinctive – and we are among the people who
consider it disagreeable – flavour, but to dismiss all Greek wines as
belonging to this category is absurd.

Like so many other European countries, Greece was occupied
by the Turks for over five hundred years. During all this time the
Greeks managed to both retain and maintain their own wine-making
traditions and methods. It must be acknowledged, even so, that the
weight of that iron Turkish hand upon them for so long is responsible in the main for their persisting, primitive, agricultural procedures.

With these facts established, let me state very plainly, Greece can
and does produce a very great number of highly drinkable non-*retsina*
table wines which range between red and white, dry and sweet.

Now to particularize a little. Firstly consider the climate; hot
and dry for a great part of the year, thus altogether very suitable
for the production of great and distinguished wines – yet *Greece
makes none* – only a quantity of sound, lower-quality wines. This,

when we contemplate the quality of her architecture, sculpture and literature is puzzling in the extreme. However, some of the best of Greek wines will be found on the island of Samos, from whence come a whole range of dry, white wines, plus a sweet *Muscat de Samos* and a very sweet red one called *Mavrodaphne*. All are very drinkable.

I must also point out here that the islanders have made a serious effort to control and protect their wines, a reform, by the way, which is both welcome and long overdue.

The Peloponnese group of islands, once joined to the mainland by the Corinth Canal, represents the most important wine-making area. This group produces over a quarter of the total output of Greek wines.

In the hilly area behind the north-west coast we find three dry white wines which are offered for sale in almost every hotel and restaurant in Athens and also in the other large towns throughout Greece. I shall now list them in the order of my personal preference, fully aware that thereafter you may well rearrange my list to suit yours; first then, *Santa Helena;* next *Antika*, and then *Demestica*. After these come two more whites called *Santa Laoura* and *Mantineia*, and finally a lusty red called *Nemea* which originates from around Corinth.

The Malvoisie grape variety was begun in the Peloponnese too, and it is generally accepted that the famous *Malmsey* wine in which the unfortunate Duke of Clarence drowned himself was this self-same wine from the Peloponnese. Modern Greek wine made from this grape is very strong, very sweet, a distant cousin to a *Jerez* Sherry. Local legend has it that the name *Mavrodaphne* was coined in the nineteenth century to commemorate a very beautiful black-haired girl named Daphne – the word *mavro* means black!

Now let us move to the mainland and the Attica district so that we can meet a really excellent light, dry, white wine called *Pallini*. I think Fanny and I must have drunk gallons of it on our many visits to Greece. It is slightly astringent and very agreeable; what is more, unlike *Retsina*, you do not feel compelled to clean your teeth half an hour later. It marries very well with a great many Greek dishes.

This part of the mainland has now got itself a new label – Continental Greece. It includes one island called Euboea, which is joined to it by a swing bridge at Chalcis, a town which gives its name to the red and white wines of the Euboean island.

Throughout Macedonia you will discover sound wines, the majority of which come from the vineyards which throng the slopes of Mount Velia to the north of that most significant name to English historians – Salonika. The best among these wines, as I think you will agree, is a red one called *Naoussa*. Thessalia also produces two sound red wines which bear the names *Rapsani* and *Amberlakia*.

The island of Crete makes a quantity of wines too. These are mostly strong, red and frankly almost exclusively drunk by the islanders. The average visitor is so absorbed in archaelogical explorations, toiling up slopes and down into valleys from dawn to dusk, and so busy debating the rather silly recent claims concerning Atlantis, to notice what they are drinking. In short, time has not been spent yet on even cursory debate and assessment of Cretan wine's vinous merits!

Rhodes and the other Dodecanese can lay claim to some more reasonable red and white wines. Likewise the charming small island of Lemnos which offers a very acceptable Muscat wine in both red and white. We spent an idyllic holiday on this famous little, virtually unspoiled, island where Rupert Brooke died on Shakespeare's birthday and during the First World War. To sit bruising the wild thyme with one's blunt end, in the shade of a fig tree, overlooking those gentian blue waters below, reflecting upon what great verse might have stemmed from that young man – had he not died when still a mere boy; and to assist reflection and contemplation with a well-chilled bottle of white Muscat wine (string-tied and dangled in the turtle stream – it's easy and effective!) is, to say the least of it, agreeable.

Before concluding, I must mention the well-known Greek *Ouzo*. This is very inexpensive to drink *in situ* and extremely potent! Please, if you have no experience of it, do not attempt to emulate the Greeks and toss it back neat – at least until you have accustomed yourselves to it. Dilute it with water and plenty of ice and discover, by experience, just what effect it has upon you and indeed whether the major effect is upon the head or the legs! The aniseed flavour is very strong and all in all I think it is best described as the poor man's *Pastis*.

The Greeks also produce a Brandy which is neither worse nor better than any other non-French Brandies. The best-known marks are *Cambus* and *Metaxa*. Look for the five- and seven-star marks on the labels. These are palatable, but scarcely merit eulogies!

THE WINES OF SWITZERLAND

This small and fascinating country has been producing wine since the tenth century. For its size Switzerland has a remarkable output, but this is not really so surprising if you accept that this industrious and commercially-minded nation utilizes every inch of ground! So much so, in respect of wine growing, that even high up in the Alps there are vineyards which are the highest plantings of grape vines in the entire world.

The Swiss claim that their sun-drenched valleys form a marvellous combination of the north and the south and that their many lakes are vast sun reflectors so that the banks are propitious for the smooth maturing of the grapes. They are very proud of their wines and maintain that the bouquet of a *Dôle du Valais* or a fine *Dézaley* can be smelt five hundred kilometres away.

Unfortunately, Swiss wines are very little known over here. This is not due to bad publicity but because the Swiss themselves are great wine drinkers and are their own chief consumers. Even so, a certain amount of very drinkable wine is now available in Britain and there is a Swiss Centre on the corner of Leicester Square and Wardour Street in London (W1) where all the best wines exported by the Swiss are available for sampling by the glass, by the carafe or by the bottle. Thus when you are next in London you can find out for yourselves how silly that old wives' tale is about Swiss wines being notoriously bad travellers.

Although practically every Canton (the equivalent to an English county) produces some wine the important areas are the Vaud, Valais, Ticino and Neuchâtel. The Vaud Canton stretches along the northern shores of Lake Léman between Geneva and Lausanne and the majority of the best growths come from this region which is divided into three districts. Lavaux lies to the east of Lausanne and gives us *Dézaley* and *St Saphorin*. It produces medium-strength dry white wines and in my opinion these are delightful, fresh and fruity, and should be numbered among the best of the Swiss dry whites, particularly those from the Clos des Abbayes vineyard. La Côte, lying west of Lausanne, is a much larger area but one that produces fairly ordinary wines. Chablais is where the river Rhône becomes broader to the east of the lake and the vineyards are situated on the northern cliff-sides. These wines, of which the best are *Yvorne* and *Aigle*, are much fuller and of greater strength than those of Lavaux.

If you travel north to the Neuchâtel region you will find dry white wine, fairly light, rather astringent and slightly *Spritzig* (a prickle rather than a sparkle). There are also some very palatable red wines from this district.

Valais is a high area in the south of the country known for its white wines. They are mostly fairly light, possess a delightful bouquet and are named after the particular types of grapes with, in some cases, the addition of brand names. The dry ones are *Humagne*, *Arvine, Amigne* and the finest of these, *Fendant*. There are also two that are reputed to be similar to French and German wines and therefore named *Hermitage* and *Johannisberg*. A sweet aperitif or after-dinner wine is also made which is aptly called *Malvoisie*. From Sion there is *Dôle*, considered by many to be the finest of the Swiss red wines.

In Italian Switzerland the wine area is called Ticino. The vines are grown in the Italian fashion, being pruned high and trained up pillars in the form of pergolas; in some instances the plants alternate throughout the vineyards with chestnut trees. While a fair amount of white wine is produced, the main growths are grapes used for red wine. Up to recent times the result was very ordinary wine for local consumption, but now a great effort is being made to improve the quality and this has been extremely successful, in particular with the Merlot grape, which provides a soft, strong red wine that is named after the grape. There is in addition a lower quality sold in large quantities called *Nastrano*.

Many of the dry white wines have a slightly flinty flavour – comparable to that of the *Pouilly-Fumé* – which comes from the Loire. This distinctive flavour caused a rather silly woman, when writing in a travel book, to state that it tasted 'as if knives had been steeped in the barrels'. So please forget this totally inaccurate statement, it is both worthless and untrue.

Amongst the best which are available here I place very high on my short list the delicate, dry white *Dézaley de Levèque*. I also recommend the *Johannisberg*, which is similar to an Alsatian wine, and one called *Fendant Soleil du Valais* which makes the very best possible partner of all to Swiss Cheese Fondues, whether you are adding in the Kirsch 'chasers' or not. There are, besides, two golden and dry wines which are worthy of your attention, *Aigle des Murailles* and *Les Perailles*. Nor must we forget an *Ermitage du Prévôt*, which is so named because of its fancied resemblance to French wines from the Rhône, and one called *Neuchâtel Œil de Perdrix*. This last can prove a pitfall for the unwary. It tastes innocuous but – in vulgar parlance – it packs a punch sufficient to make any but the hard-headed pretty tipsy if they refresh themselves with it over-generously, so drink cautiously, at least on first consumption.

Take advice, please, and drink Swiss wines while they are fairly young. As a general rule they do not age well. When choosing red wines use this final short list as a safe guide for beginners. . . *Chanteauvieux, Pinot Noir, Salvagnin* (or *Genfersee*) from the borders of Lake Léman, and *Merlot* which is similar to its sturdy Italian counterpart.

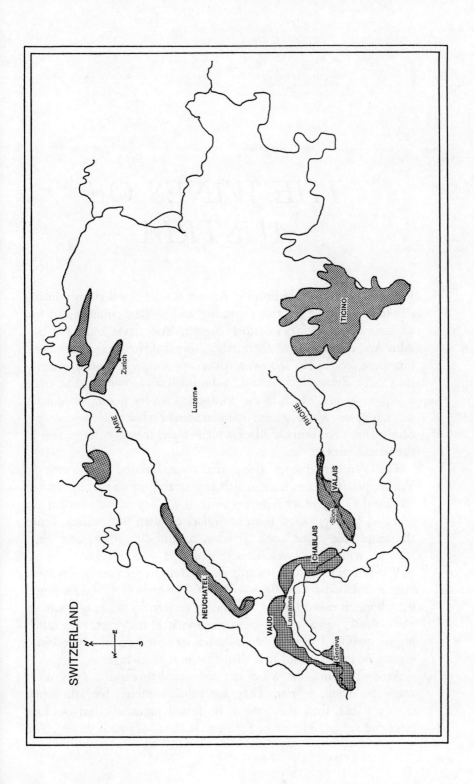

SWITZERLAND

N

W—E

S

AARE

Zurich

Luzerne

RHONE

NEUCHATEL

VALAIS

Sion

CHABLAIS

VAUD

Lausanne

Geneva

TICINO

THE WINES OF AUSTRIA

In the days of the Old Empire, Austria was a large wine-producing country, but by 1918 this charming and elegant country had lost all her eastward vineyards to Hungary, Yugoslavia and Trentino-Alto Adige. She is now, regrettably, very little larger than Scotland. She produces today less wine than any other European country save only Switzerland and Czechoslovakia. However, the stress is still on *quality*. Much of the production is very good, particularly in respect of white wines; these comprise about eighty-five per cent of the total output, all of which comes from grapes grown in the remaining eastward vineyards.

The Wachau district along the river Danube north-west of Vienna produces the wine which is probably more widely sold in Britain than any other Austrian wine. It is a dry white with a slight sparkle (*Spritzig*) called *Wachau-Schluck* or often just *Schluck*. From the same area come both *Trifalter*, a semi-dry white, and *Edel-fräulein*, which is a sweet dessert wine.

Weinvietel extends eastwards from Krem to the Czechoslovakian border and includes the Vienna district. The main type of wine found hereabouts is called *Gruner Veltliner*, a very fruity white one which, like *Schluck*, has a natural effervescence. It is, however, of a much higher quality. It is very often drawn straight from the barrel into a mug or tumbler and it is then that it is at its best.

Around Vienna the wines are not suited to export. They must really be drunk *in situ*. They are usually offered for sale when freshly made, then they are to be found in numberless outdoor cafés and cellars. The name for these is *Heurige* (young wines). The proprietors of these rustic establishments hang pine branches or straw crowns outside their premises to indicate that the new wines are ready. This is when the local population and many tourists pour in to drink and be gay together. The wines are frequently served in a traditional glass mug and always there is a background of music. After a short while everyone begins to sing, and indeed the new wine is not considered to have been honourably celebrated unless the revellers are quite hoarse on the following morning. A knowledge of the language is not necessary to share in and enjoy such simple revels.

It has always been a mystery to me that a nation which has suffered as much as Austria can remain so gay, yet they have, and their wines possess similar gay characteristics. The combination is irresistible. We spent last New Year's Eve in a small Austrian restaurant in London with a party of friends and had a most hilarious night. In moments strangers were visiting each other's tables, which is something of an achievement with the reserved English. It was reminiscent of many winter parties in Austria – it became in fact a small corner of that charming country, in England.

Baden, to the south of Vienna, is the name of that famous spa where everyone drinks the waters. Indeed, it is said there is so much warm spring water drunk that it is necessary to have a great deal of wine available in order to maintain a proper balance. From this district come wines whose names are familiar to most people – the *Gumpoldskircheners*. There are several, all white, strong and full-bodied, but with a delicate flavour. The majority are slightly sweet. In addition, a few red wines are made a little further south at Bad Vosland.

Then comes Burgenland, which comprises the area round Lake Neusiedel and extends somewhat farther south. The wines hereabouts are nearly all semi-dry whites, *Ruster Greiner, Ruster Satz*, to cite two, and to make mention of the reds, a *Rust Limberger* which I found to be quite agreeable.

Finally, around Graz right in the south, white wines are produced of a somewhat similar nature to the Yugoslavian *Lutomers*, but in my opinion they are emphatically less appealing.

A word of warning to the traveller. An Austrian wine list is often rather puzzling the name by which the wine is known is not always mentioned. Sometimes only the place is quoted like *Wachauer*, sometimes only the name of the grape and yet again perhaps only the name of the village! However, if you find wines listed with the village name followed by the vineyard such as *Durnsteiner Stifts-garten* you may rest assured that you have encountered quality. In any case, this scarcely rates as worrying. The majority of holiday wines are more often than not just that – holiday drinks. It is also the custom all over Austria for a wineglass to be less than half-filled with wine and then just topped up with soda water – no comment!

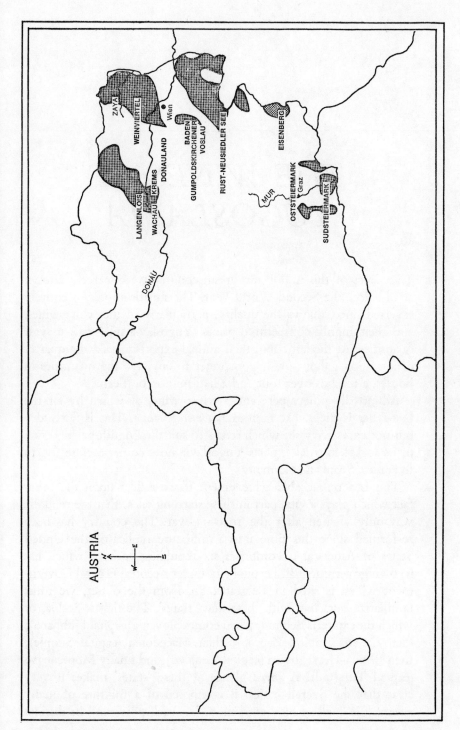

AUSTRIA

WEINVIERTEL
ZAYA
DONAULAND
Wien
BADEN
GUMPOLDSKIRCHENER
VOSLAU
RUST-NEUSIEDLER SEE
EISENBERG
LANGENLOIS
WACHAU
KREMS
MUR
OSTSTEIERMARK
Graz
SUDSTEIERMARK
DONAU

D

THE WINES OF YUGOSLAVIA

The wines of this middle-European country were scarcely known at all before the Second World War. The situation today is entirely reversed since, due to the quality, particularly of the white wines, and their highly competitive prices, Yugoslavia now sells us vast quantities. At the last count their annual exports exceeded a quarter of a million gallons or, if you prefer to envisage the quantities in bottles, a total of over four and a half million bottles!

Admittedly ninety per cent is white wine, of which by far the best-seller is their now famous *Lutomer Riesling*. This is fairly dry but not excessively so, which seems to suit the English palate down to its socks! In total exports Yugoslavia now comes a close fourth to France, Spain and Germany.

This is a remarkable achievement if we reflect upon the other fact which plays a vital part in these startling sales: that the republic was only created after the 1939-45 war. The country has been re-formed since this time into a miniature replica of the United States of America. It comprises six republics; each of which has its own government and capital city under a central Federal Government which is sited in Belgrade. So, from the outset, we must familiarize ourselves with these new 'states'. The first is Serbia, of which the capital is Belgrade; then comes Slovenia (capital Ljubljana); then Croatia (capital Zagreb); then Macedonia (capital Skopje); then Bosnia-Herzegovina (capital Sarajevo), and finally Montenegro (capital Titograd). A mere glance at these 'states' makes it very clear that the overall nation is composed of a mixture of many nationalities – all of Slav extraction, but each possessing its distinct national characteristics and costumes. There are, too, as can be equally readily understood, not only four languages, Serbian, Croatian, Slovene and Macedonian, but also two alphabets! When we examine the religions of these various peoples we find they include Catholics, Muslims and members of the Eastern Orthodox Christian faith, to which we must also add very important Protestant and Jewish minorities.

Like all the central and south-eastern European countries the viticultural history dates back to Greek, Roman and Ottoman Turkish times.

Due to these many racial differences and the geographical location, which causes climatic conditions which vary from sub-tropical in the south to a far less temperate climate in the north, the wines differ greatly in quality and character. They vary from the very delicate, fragrant and fresh northern wines to the much heavier, stronger, more often sweet ones of the south.

Although the industry is, naturally, state-run there is a minimum of government interference in the actual working operations. In this context it is an interesting fact that something like ninety-five per cent of the vineyards are in the hands of peasant owners. Thus they have created a combination of communist and capitalist systems which works extremely well.

There are six main wine-growing areas, so now that we have set the scene we will examine each in turn. First comes northern Slovenia which is far and away the most important in terms of quality, though it only produces ten per cent of the total output of wine. Owing to the mountainous nature of the terrain the vineyards are either spread out on the coastal plain or else along the river valleys. The yield is mostly of white wines closely resembling German ones in taste, bouquet and colour, but, as they possess a far higher alcoholic content, these Slovenian wines have greater stability in bottle and are much more even in quality. The best-known district is Lutomer-Ormoz and the most popular wine the *Lutomer Riesling*, dry as I have already explained, but not too dry for the average palate. I would categorize this as a wine that can either be drunk as an aperitif or throughout a meal.

In the higher part of the region we find the renowned vineyards of *Jeruzalem*, so called because the location constituted a resting place for Crusaders travelling to and from the Holy Wars. The wines hereabouts are fruity, fresh and well balanced. There are other excellent white ones too, including *Sylvaner*, very full and fruity, *Traminer*, more robust and aromatic, constituting the aristocrat of the *Lutomer* range, and some beautifully dry, crisp *Sauvignons* and *Rulanders*.

From the surroundings of Kapela Spa comes a very strong sweet spätlese wine named *Radgonska Ranina* or 'Tiger Milk', though it has just about as close an affiliation to the animal as the Hungarian 'Bull's Blood' has to bulls! All these wines will be found in the districts which lie north of the Drava river. You will come across some very good vineyards to the south of this river where production is of white wines and the purely local *Halozan* wines. Vast quantities of this latter are consumed *in situ*.

The moderately hilly terrain on the banks of the Sava river yields grapes for red, white and rosé (or *Siller*) wines of slightly lower quality. Nevertheless, these too are very palatable, of which the best among the rosé is *Cvicek*, light in colour and low in alcoholic content. You will also come across a dark red, strong one called *Metliska Crnina*. These are all sold and consumed locally. In the western part of Slovenia there are several wine regions like Brda which produce golden-coloured, full, dry wines. From Goriska comes another local white wine made from a blend of several types of grapes which bears the name *Vipavac*. This wine was reputed in the sixteenth century to be an aphrodisiac. I suggest that it is no more than a red wine which would improve greatly if it were allowed to mature for several years! In addition there is a medium-red one – *Kraski Teran* – which is worthy of, at least, a tasting.

Moving into Croatia, the bulk of the production is found to be of white wines. The better-quality ones come from the north in the Sava and Danube valleys, while the lesser ones emanate from the eastern districts. They are all bigger and stronger than the Slovenian wines and less suitable for our market, yet surprisingly these dry wines form the basis of a very good sweet dessert wine called *Prosek*. However, the duty is high for us on all this range, for which we can blame very high alcoholic content!

In the Istrian peninsula and its surrounding islands you will find a number of full-bodied red wines and sweet dessert wines which, I submit, are really most palatable drunk in their places of origin. Anyway, very little is exported, for these Istrian wines are bad travellers. You can also find a ruby-coloured dessert wine here about which the less said the better!

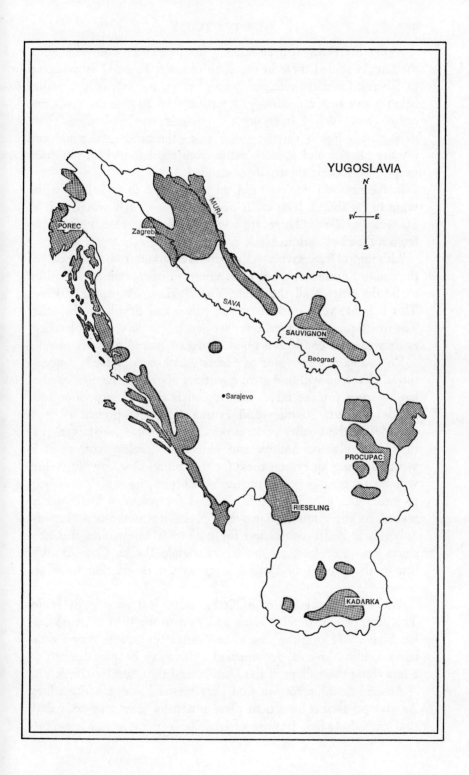

YUGOSLAVIA

N
W—E
S

POREC

MURA

Zagreb

SAVA

SAUVIGNON

Beograd

•Sarajevo

PROCUPAC

RIESELING

KADARKA

Along the Dalmatian coastline vines have been cultivated since the Greeks settled there in the sixth century. From Dubrovnik up to Sibenik there are reds, whites and rosés, the best of the whites being a dry one called *Pǒsip*. I recommend among the rosés one called *Opol*. When it comes to reds – all are full-bodied, dark, strong and slightly on the sweet side – the producers' pride and joy are *Dingacs* and *Postups*, made from the late-picked, sun-dried grapes. Both these are strictly controlled.

In the northern region right up to Kvarner there is little white wine to be found. The main production is of red wines such as *Plavinas* and *Babíc*. There are also a number of rosé wines made from a blend of various black grapes.

Although Herzegovina only produces about two per cent of the country's wines it boasts what a number of connoisseurs consider to be the best of all the white Yugoslavians – *Mostarska Zilavka*. This is light, very smooth on the palate and dryish in character. The small quantities of red wine are generally reserved for blending, as they are not considered good enough to stand on their own.

Vojvodina is a province of Serbia which is completely autonomous. Here you will find great quantities of grapes, the majority being reserved for the table. The region is divided into three sub-regions – Banat, Subotiča and Fruska Gora. At present none is notable for the quality of its products. I do know, however, that they are under continuous and extensive development, so it is worth keeping an eye on these for the future. One day Vojvodina will be producing good, medium-quality wines which will help to satisfy the growing world demand for palatable lower-priced wines! At the moment Banat is a promising white-wine region; Subotiča is under cultivation for both reds and whites and here again we must look to the future, while Fruska Gora is only just in the process of turning over to the production of white wines.

The wine-growing area of Serbia starts just outside Belgrade. This area, which stretches south and west to the Rumanian border, has been cultivating the vine since Roman times. It is very mountainous, like Slovenia, so vineyard cultivation is again limited to a line along the valleys of the Danube and the Moravia rivers.

Around Smederevo you find very reasonable dry white wines. As you go farther south, so these gradually give way to a dark rosé named *Ružica*. Beware of it! Like so many rosés, it appears

fairly innocuous, but in fact has a kick like several of those prover-
bial mules.

As we travel on we find that these rosé regions merge into ones
producing red wine in another autonomous Serbian province
hereabouts called Kosmet. This adjoins Albania and has a long
vinous history with an almost clean break in its records deriving
from and running through the time of the phylloxera tragedy and
continuing until twelve years ago when a large-scale development
and re-planting began again. Now, as before, quite a healthy red
wine production has been redeveloped together with a small
output of white.

Macedonia produces mostly red wines and the whites are very
limited. Nor are they of any particular merit; indeed I do not consider
any of them are worth bothering about! So let us, as Mr Sam
Goldwyn said, 'include them out' – at present.

Finally there is the little province of Montenegro, the romantic
musical-comedy region which alas does not live up to its colourful
reputation at all when it comes to wines. These can at best only be
called 'plonk', best drunk in Montenegro, and as the late M. André
L. Simon commented in another vinous context, 'thirst-quenching
and forgotten immediately after drinking'!

Having studied the leading importers lists which offer only
the reasonably priced and very worthwhile wines, I am surprised
not only at the variety but also – after tasting – by their quality,
so I shall end this chapter with a brief summary of the most readily
available ones adding in my own, purely personal comments.

Lutomer Sauvignon, the driest, is excellent with fish, also *Lutomer
Sylvaner* which is demi-sec and a good all-rounder.

Lutomer Riesling, dryish, but not as dry as the *Sauvignon*, is the
most popular of all.

Lutomer Traminer, demi-sec but fuller and able to stand up to
most dishes like some of the Germans.

Lutomer Luternes, a sweet dessert wine which, as the name implies,
has a similarity to *Sauternes*.

Château Fleur Blanc, very sweet and heady.

Ranina Radgone (Tiger Milk), medium sweet and a good wine
to drink on its own between meals.

Beli Burgundec, the poor man's white Burgundy, is very palatable.

Of the reds, there are four, all to my mind much better than the average low-priced ones from other countries. They are:

Burgomer Burgundec, with a resemblance to a light Burgundy but slightly sweeter.

Cabernet, a light mild wine.

Pinot Noir (Istrian), full-bodied and heady.

Castle d'Almain, a recent addition, lightish, fairly dry and extremely pleasant.

I also recommend:

Sans Thorn, a mild, light rosé.

Maraska, Cherry Brandy which I beg you to try.

Slivovica (Serbian Plum Brandy), also worth a tasting.

THE WINES OF HUNGARY

Hungary is best known in this country for its world-famous sweet wine *Tokay*, yet this is only one very small part of this country's overall production. In terms of quality (not quantity), despite its smallness, Hungary is one of the leading wine-producing countries of the world, something that, even now, few people realize.

Let us first examine *Tokay*. In the good old days the most famous was the *Imperial Tokay*. Certain of the finest vineyards were then part of the original Habsburg domains and the Emperors reserved the wines for very special gifts to the privileged few. The name derives from the town of Tokay (Tokaj) which is situated in the Carpathian foothills. *Tokay Essenz* was always fabulous in price and quality but is no longer available since the communists came to power. This Imperial Tokay was made from juice squeezed from the grapes by their own weight, with no added pressure. Even nowadays the best *Tokay* is expensive, but I have included it in this book because of its interesting history and method of making and also because very drinkable *Tokays* are still available which are within reach of the average purse.

Tokay at its greatest is comparable with the foremost *Sauternes* and the leading German dessert wines. It is also said to possess very special medicinal qualities. Hungarians insist it only just falls short of being able to raise the dead!

It is made by a very special process which, like the *Sauternes*, is dependent upon the *Pourriture noble* or 'noble rot' which is explained on p. 26. The vintage begins late – traditionally on St Simon's Day (the 28th October). The rotten grapes, called *Aszú*, are trodden very carefully so that the pips are not crushed. In some modernized areas this traditional treading has been replaced by presses. The residue of pips are then hand-picked from the 'must' and squeezed until they form something rather similar to dough. It is this which is placed in small butts (*Puttonyos*). The remainder of the grapes – ripe, but not attacked by the 'rot' – are then collected, pressed and the juice placed in smaller-than-usual barrels, each containing 30/35 gallons and called *Gönc*.

At this point you may wonder why I am being so technical. Please bear with me and you will, I hope, understand. When the grapes are in a *Gönc* some of the dough is then added. The quality of the end product depends on the quantity of this addition. Look at a bottle of *Tokay* and you will see on the label the statement 'three, four or five *Puttonyos*'. Sometimes this is abbreviated to *Putts*. This is the treatment for fine *Tokays* which, once they are in bottle, will keep for centuries; in fact wines of the seventeenth century have been opened fairly recently and found to be in excellent condition.

Of course there is a more common type of *Tokay* called *Szamorodni* which is made from the whole bunches of grapes, some rotten, some just ripe. According to the proportion of these to each other, the end product will be either a dry or a sweet wine.

Viniculture in Hungary has existed for many centuries, in fact vine-stocks were probably planted by the Celts who were said to be connoisseurs of good wine, but methodical planting and growing only came into existence during the Roman rule. Since then it has had many ups and downs caused by the many migrants that have passed through during the centuries, but viniculture has always managed to survive and today represents a flourishing Hungarian industry.

The country is divided into five areas of varying size. The largest is the Great Hungarian Plain which extends from Kisvärda in the north-east to Budapest in the west, then south to the border near Mohacs and along the southern frontier adjoining Yugoslavia and Rumania. This area produces sixty-five per cent of all the wines of the country. The northern vineyards yield lightish white and rosé wines, dessert wines and the basic wines of the Champagne type. The south yields white, red and dessert wines, the proportions being seventy-four per cent white to twenty per cent red and only six per cent dessert. Much of the soil is sandy, so particular care has to be taken in the selection of the type of grape most suited to it.

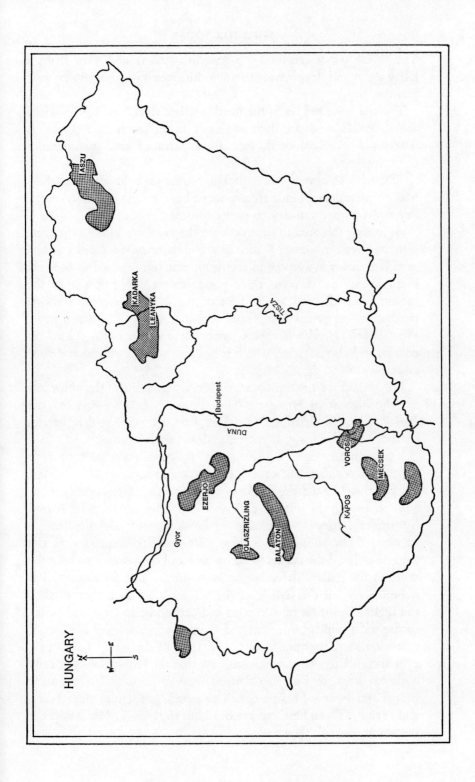

The white wines are mostly a greenish yellow and vary from a fairly astringent dryish wine to a smooth sweet one of high alcoholic content.

The red wine grapes in the north are late ripening and the wines aromatic. The rosés are light and fresh. In the south the red wine is fierce and ruby-coloured, but more balanced and undoubtedly more mellow.

There is also a very large sparkling wine trade around Budafok. More than a dozen kinds are produced here, ranging from the very dry and the medium-dry to sweet Muscat-flavoured.

Adjoining this area to the north are the northern Hungarian wine districts stretching from Kosice in the west to Nove Zamky in the east. If we start at Hatvan in the south-east and proceed to Miskolc in the west, we traverse three good wine areas: first comes the mountainous districts at the foot of the Matra mountains which produce white wines like *Abasar* which is a dry full-bodied wine, then *Debrői Hàrslevelü*, spicy, sweetish and greenish yellow in colour, and also *Muscate*, which is both powerfully strong and very sweet.

Proceeding west, we encounter Eger, where some of the vineyards are the highest in Hungary. This district is best known for the *Egri Bikavér*, 'Bull's Blood', a robust, dark red wine which marries so well with the many highly spiced Hungarian dishes.

It may amuse you to know that the Hungarians take great pains to ensure that there is not even a remote connection with bulls. The story is that in 1562 the Turks laid siege to the fortress of Eger for a whole month. In spite of their vastly superior numbers supported by artillery, they were unable to break in and take the Pasha's standard from above the fortress. When the commander of the fortress ordered the cellars to be opened and the women to take the wine to the gallant defenders, these women – not for nothing has it been said that the female of the species is more dangerous than the male – also took up weapons and carried boiling tar and water to the walls which both men and women emptied over the Turks, renewing their energies from the strength of the wine. The Turks, ever inclined towards mysticism, saw that the Hungarians not only gathered strength but also that, as they emptied their cups, their beards and swords became red. This struck terror into their hearts and crying, 'These heathens are drinking the blood of bulls and the bulls will toss us', they fled.

Although most noted for its red wines, this district also produces some very palatable white wines, notably *Leányka*, a smooth, honey-tasting greenish-white wine. There are also a number of dry white wines produced.

Finally, there is the Bükkalja region which has only started to develop during the past twenty years and is now producing a quantity of mostly dry white wine. The area is also turning its attention to the production of sparkling wines.

The third area is Northern Transdanubia, which lies to the north-west and the west of the country. If we first journey south-west we come to Lake Balaton and on its northern shores find a very important district for good fruity golden wines with a touch of sweetness, such as *Balatoni Furmint* (from a grape unique to Hungary) and *Balatoni Riesling*. These make good aperitif wines to be drunk between meals, but they are also capable of making good partners to a number of dishes. However, the best of these lakeland wines are those of Badacsony, of which undoubtedly the driest is *Kéknyeld*, rather acid, smoky and strong; A more elegant one, not quite so dry, is the early-bottled *Olaszrizling*; then there is the golden *Szürkebarat*. Close by we find the Balatonfüred-csopak district, with its varying types of white wine, ranging from dryish greeny whites to mellow old-gold dessert wines. By comparison, the Somlo region is very small; the wine produced here needs at least three years to mature. These wines are not sold under individual names and can rarely be bought by the casual customer – local consumers buy straight from the cellars. Even so, you may be lucky enough to be invited to partake of a glass of this old-gold liquid which is a unique experience.

There is a fable here too and it serves to illustrate the size of the region. There was once a rabbit who taunted a lioness on not being as fertile as she had been. The lioness replied, 'It may be true that I only have one cub a year, but that is a lion!'

Next we have the Mór region, producing mostly slightly acid, full-bodied white wines with a certain roughness which is characteristic in this area. Finally we have the red wine from the Sopron centre, the best of which, I submit, is *Sopron Kékfrankos*. It is a rich dark ruby colour and rather spicy; this flavour derives from the special wooden barrels in which it is matured.

The fourth area is Southern Transdanubia in the south-west. If you are visiting this part of the country and journeying from

Budapest, do take time off to visit the fisherman's inn at Duna-kömlöd (*Dunakömlödi Halaszcsarda*), this is renowned for its fish soup. Proceed thence to the mountainous wine district of Mecsek to sample some fine, dry white wines which are fairly strong and have a distinct bouquet of mignonette – in an exceptional vintage they also produce a natural dessert wine called *Mecsek Rizling* or *Pécsi Olasrizling*. Moving in again to the district of Villány-Siklós, we get both red and white wines. The red from the *Oporto* grape is aromatic and deep-coloured, the *Kadarka* a ruby red, the *Burgundi*, dark and robust, the *Médoc Noir* dark but not so heavy, while the *Cabernet* is pleasantly rough. The Szekszárd region offers both red and white wines which are somewhat similar in character, while the wines from the south of Lake Balaton are admired mostly for such specific ones as *Chasselas, Ssabagyöngye* and *Cardinal Rosé*.

The fifth area is Tokaj in the north, the home of *Tokay*, with which I dealt at the beginning of this chapter.

In addition to their table wines, the Hungarians have a thriving industry in spirits such as *Barack Pálinka* (Apricot Brandy), *Szilva-pálinka* (Plum Brandy), *Cseresznyapálinka* (Kirsch), *Hubertus*, a bitter-sweet orange flavour liqueur, *Mecsek*, an aperitif and Cherry Brandy. Most of these are obtainable in England at very reasonable prices.

Many of the Hungarian table wines are exported to this country, and I can recommend to you in particular *Egri Bikavér* (Bull's Blood), the *Cabernet* from Hajos, which constitutes an excellent bargain among the reds, and, in the range of whites, *Balatoni Riesling, Balatoni Furmint, Mori Dry, Debrői Hàrslevelü*. These are all in the lower price bracket as are several *Tokays* of three, four and five *Puttonyos*.

In a slightly higher price range, but still well within the average purse, look out for *Badacsonyi Zoldszilvani* and *Badacsonyi Kéknyelu*. This latter is a full, dry wine with a slight resemblance to a Burgundy Likewise you should try the similar but bigger and richer *Badacsonyi Szürkebarat*.

THE WINES OF
BULGARIA

On all counts Bulgaria is virtually a non-starter with the average
Englishman when he is pursuing the wine trail. General knowledge
of that country begins and ends with the vague acceptance that
Bulgaria is a Balkan country which lies behind the Iron Curtain,
that it is very poor and more than a little depressing. You may
therefore be a bit surprised to learn that you really should be
hearing a great deal more about the vinous activities of Bulgaria in
the immediate future. It has been my pleasure to indulge in a number of tastings of modestly priced Bulgarian wines in the last few
weeks before writing this chapter and I am frankly agreeably
impressed by them.

Bulgaria is basically a peasant country; the word *Bulgar* means a
ploughing peasant or a cultivator. It is a mountainous country too,
but between these mountains lie a great number of fertile valleys
which have been turned into market gardening centres and which
produce large quantities of wheat, tomatoes, pimentoes and other
vegetables. The vine, of course, has been cultivated here since before
Roman times, but, because the Bulgarians were under Turkish
Muslim rule from 1396 until they gained a small measure of independence in 1878, commercial wine production was simply not
possible. Under the communist regime vast changes have, of course,
been made. What concerns us is that today Bulgaria is producing
a large quantity of wine (some fifty million gallons of it annually)
and the Bulgarians are now exporting as much as eighty per cent
of these wines to other countries in many parts of the world. All
the work is done under the strictest supervision and in large co-

operatives which are equipped with modern machinery throughout, in fact they employ the most up-to-date methods.

The main wine production is in the north in the province of Trnovo. The town of Sukhindal is particularly famous for its red wines made from the Gamay grape. Then at nearby Povlikani about twenty-five million kilos of grapes are pressed for these wines annually. The majority of the dry white and the sweet dessert wines come from around these parts. In and around Lyaskovits we can also find a very large number of sparkling wines, about twenty-five per cent of which are made according to the Champagne method. Then there is a dark red wine produced from Mavried grapes which comes from an area south of the Ljaskovec province and in the Plovdiv region.

Main types with which I think you will wish to concern yourselves among the white wines are *Dimiat*, which is categorized as a white wine but is actually greenish yellow in colour and very dry on the palate, another, *Misket*, is rather fuller, white and not quite so dry, then there is *Sonnenküste* dry and white and another interesting dry white wine called *Chardonnay*. Among the reds I would cite *Mavrud*, dark red in colour, a very lusty and full-bodied wine; *Gamza* is very fruity and even darker red in colour; *Melnik*, which suits some, is a light claret type and *Kadarka* a somewhat unusual, sweet, red wine. There is also a deep rosé called *Pamid*; this should be drunk very young, it is pleasant, thirst-quenching and of absolutely no vinous importance whatever. Then we come to a sparkling wine called *Iskra*; this is better, I suggest, if drunk when young. It comes in three categories: *Iskra Dry, Iskra Semi-Dry* and *Iskra Red*, this last is the only really sweet one.

Now you will not I think find it easy to credit that Bulgaria is now the biggest exporter of wines in bottle – bigger than France, bigger even than Italy! In addition, this country is growing quantities of wine for export to Britain in cask. The four main wines in this category are *Cabernet*, a medium-full red wine; *Gamza*, a dark red wine with the lustiness but not, of course, the distinction of a Burgundy; *Chardonnay* which is very dry and white, and *Sylvaner* which is a medium-dry and quite fruity, white wine. All these are very modest in price and to my mind represent really good value for money in these hard times. To particularize for a moment I think you will most like the *Sylvaner* among the white wines, but will also be very agreeably impressed by the reds.

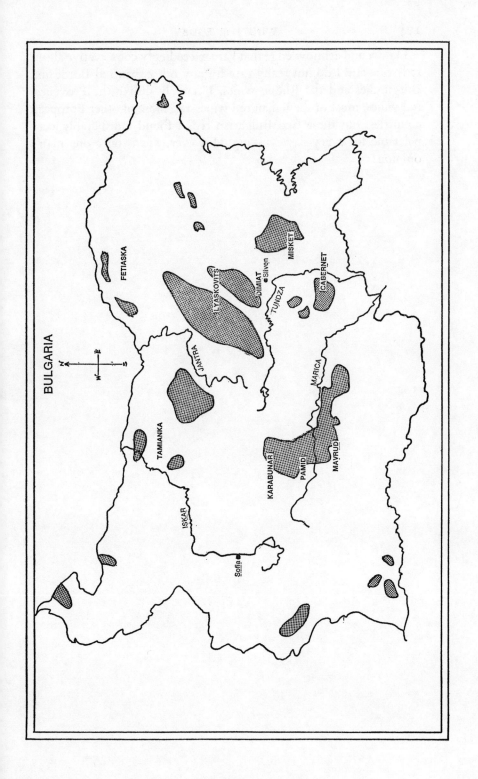

I know and acknowledge that I am exceedingly conservative about red wine and I do not really care for any other than red Bordeaux, Burgundies and the Rhône wines. I actively dislike the Provençal red wines, most of the Italian red wines and those of other European countries, but these two Bulgarian reds I found indisputably very palatable for every-day drinking. However, this is only one man's opinion!

THE WINES OF
RUMANIA

Rumania is another middle European country which lays claim to
an extremely ancient tradition of wine growing. There is abundant
evidence of wine making before the Roman occupation of A.D. 101
and indeed they claim to trace it back to about 3000 B.C. Since they
freed themselves from the Turks in 1878 their wine industry has
gone forward by leaps and bounds so that now they are estimated
to be about the fourth biggest producers in the world.

The industry is to all intents and purposes under state control, with
large well-equipped and highly organized farms and co-operatives,
and it is evident that, although they are re-planting, the intention
is not so much to extend their existing acreage as to improve the
quality of what is being grown. The climate varies from hot in the
east to temperate in the west and the vineyards are almost
equally divided between the plains, tablelands and mountainous
regions.

The most easterly vineyards are those of Dobrudja, near the
Bulgarian border and of Constanta behind the port on the Black
Sea. These wines are white and sweet; principally used as dessert
wines, they are quite good but not likely to appeal to the average
British palate.

The Obesti region south of Moldavia is the largest Rumanian
wine-producing area. It makes large quantities of ordinary white
wine for local consumption and smaller quantities of red and white
of much better quality.

Adjoining is the small region of Cotnari. There we find what is
reputed to be the best white wine – *Grusă De Cotnari*. It is a heavy,

sweet, white wine, and can best be described as a humble relation of the great Hungarian *Tokay*.

North of the capital city of Bucharest and in the Carpathian foothills is the Dealul Mare district whence come some very powerful white wines. There too you will discover some of the best red wines which I have found drinkable as modestly priced products.

Transylvania, which lies between the Transylvanian Alps and the Carpathians, gives us several white wines which are exported not only to England, but also to Japan. Probably the best of these are *Tirnave Perla*, a medium-sweet, light wine, and *Rulander* which is somewhat sweeter.

The Dragasani district which lies along the west bank of the river Olt has interesting wines to contribute. Both the reds and whites are made from native grape stocks for purely home consumption, these are much better-quality wines than those which are produced, both reds and whites, specifically for export.

Amid the fertile plains of the south-west we find a number of rivers including the Olt. Here the Romans used to produce red wines and good-quality ones were made right up to 1884, when the area, like most of Europe, was devastated by the dreaded phylloxera blight. These devastated vineyards have only been re-planted very recently and already a red *Cabernet* and a rosé from Sadova can be obtained in England. They are worth trying.

There are a few other wine-producing areas, but none of them merit our attention as yet. Who knows, though, maybe in time this state of affairs could change fairly rapidly through the efforts being made to improve the 'viniculture'. Then, perhaps we shall be able to sit at our own dinner tables and debate the merits of 'travelling' wines from this region of Rumania.

Nor is this small tally adequate if I fail to mention two Rumanian fruit Brandies. One is called *Tzuica*, it tastes of plums and almonds, the other is *Slibouitza*, as it is precisely the same as Yugoslavian *Slivovica*, which I described on p. 94, so I will abstain from repeating myself here.

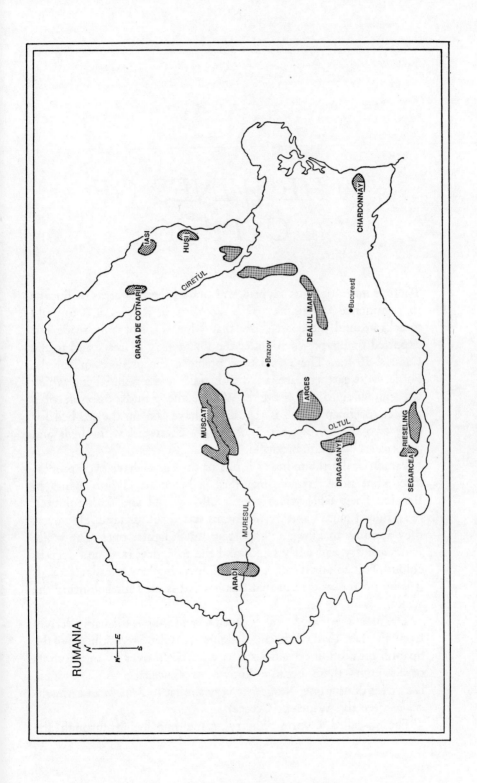

RUMANIA

CHARDONNAY

IASI

HUSI

GRASA DE COTNARI

CIRETUL

DEALUL MARE

•Bucuresti

•Brazov

ARGES

OLTUL

MUSCAT

DRAGASANY

SEGARCEA RIESELING

MURESUL

ARAD

THE WINES OF
CYPRUS

There is no doubt that Cyprus was one of the first areas of Europe to commence viticulture. The recovery of amphorae from old wrecks around the coast show that wine was not only made but exported to Egypt when under the Pharaohs, to Greece and to the Caesars' Rome. These ancient containers, the predecessors of the bottle, were earthenware jars with handles and a pointed end which was pushed into the ground. We are the proud possessors of a perfect specimen which is reputed to have lain on the sea-bed for over two thousand years. It is deeply encrusted with shells and tiny stones but quite beautiful.

Paradoxically the industry is one of the last to have been modernized, but nowadays a great deal is heard of Cyprus wines in Britain. Their table wines consist of very full and dark-coloured reds, full of tannin and by no means suited to our taste. However, they are now making and exporting much lighter ones. The white wines are dry and fairly fruity and the rosé, dry, fresh and deep in colour. This colour is called *kokkineli* meaning 'cochineal', although it is by no means certain that this is what is used for colouring the wines.

The most renowned wine is called *Commandaria*; the name derives from the fact that when the Knights Templar were killed by the Spanish Inquisition certain districts were taken over by the Knights of St John – these became known as *Commanderies*. The wine is a sweet dessert one, altogether very similar to *Malaga* and *Mavrodaphne* (see the Wines of Greece).

The so-called Cyprus 'Sherry' came into being through the

tendency of the white wines to 'maderize' (turn a brownish colour and develop a musty smell) in the heat. They have now developed *flor* (a name used for the film of yeast forming on the surface) Sherry and their dry ones are comparable with South African ones at similar prices.

THE WINES OF
NORTH AFRICA

MOROCCO

Moroccan wines date back to Roman times and, as in England when we were occupied by the Romans, so in Morocco the Romans initiated the planting of wines, the building of terraces and the cultivation of the grape. They gave Morocco the name of *Tingita Mauretania*. The real wine production of today owes its initiation, however, to yet another occupation. In 1907 the French occupied Casablanca and found that three or four of their compatriots had already planted about twenty-five acres of vines yielding wine grapes. These were followed by more European invaders and in four short years there were more than sixty-five thousand of them. Many planted vineyards, but, though they were wine drinkers, they had to import their wines in these early days until there were pressings from their harvests to yield enough to drink. Most of these imports came from Spain, very cheap and rather disagreeable, but by 1916 there were over eight hundred acres under French cultivation on Moroccan soil. These were situated around Meknes, Rabat and in the Sebououjda valley. When the First World War ended Europeans began pouring in, so great was the influx that by 1936 a quarter of a million of them had settled in Morocco and the vineyard acreage had risen to over thirty-six thousand. This represented a yield of around twelve million gallons of wine per annum. At this time, of course, no Moroccan wines were exported and a large quantity of wine was still being brought in from both Spain and France.

The first exports were made in 1933 and it is interesting to note that the gradually dwindling imports had ceased altogether by 1934. This is an extraordinary situation when you realize that the Moroccans themselves never drink alcohol – it is against their religion. Therefore this vast quantity was consumed by non-Moroccans in Morocco and must have represented the highest consumption *per capita* of any country in the world. There were, of course, three contributary factors: the climate which is hot and dry was conducive to thirst; there was an enormous shortage of water fit for Europeans to drink, and, constituting the prime allure, neither growers nor sellers paid any tax, any licence or any other dues. Naturally all this progress which occurred between the years 1924 and 1931 was due to the support and encouragement given by the French rulers. It was they who established a number of modern co-operatives. Among the best were the two near Casablanca, the ones at Meknes, Fez, Rabat (you might like to pay a visit when holidaying in these areas) and the little group scattered over the eastern part of the country in and around Beni-Snassen and Ait Souala.

Between 1935 and 1945 the European population rose to half a million. Unfortunately, during the Second World War it became impossible to obtain the necessary machinery for planting new vineyards in virgin soil, or indeed to get the remedies essential for combating the various diseases which attack vines. So imports began again, but the difficulties in the way of these were so great that eventually rationing had to be introduced. After the Second World War enormous efforts were made: a number of co-operatives were established at Taza, Oujda, Marchand, Soul-et-Tieta, Rharb, and Sidi-Slimene which between them raised the vineyard acreage yet again and by 1957 this had risen to 172,000 acres.

When you realize that the rainfall is extremely limited this really does represent an extraordinary achievement. As you all know, Morocco later established her independence. In consequence the number of European settlers decreased with, in some cases, somewhat indecent haste. Despite this, and with the concomitant reduction in liquor consumption, the astute Moroccans can boast today some 166,000 acres under vine cultivation which proves what a really splendid job had been done. Alas, practically all modern methods are mechanical and the old, traditional, manual work is now almost extinct.

So what of the wine itself? To give you a comparison with which you must nearly all be familiar, the wines of Morocco may be likened to those of France's Provence. The reds are generous, some of them are rich, many are fairly well balanced, but none of them could advance any claims to subtlety. The rosés are fruity, clean and lively and as in Provence these make the best drinking in a hot climate. The whites are frankly a little on the heavy side.

Now let us be a bit more specific. On my most recent visit to Morocco I drank a number of native wines and I made a list of the ones which I thought were exceptionally drinkable. Try them when you are next on holiday in this lovely country and try to have a look at one of the co-operatives if you find yourself in any adjacent region which makes such a visit practical.

I chose the red wines of *Chaudsoleil, Valpierre* and *Thaleb*, the dry white wines of *Oustalet*, a *Blanc de Blanc* of *Berkane* and a very oddly described 'grey' wine called *Boulaouane* which, despite its description, I believe you will find the most agreeable of all.

Finally, because, as you probably realize, Moroccan sweetmeats are very sweet indeed, you really should add in, for teaming with these Moroccan specialities, their sweet dessert wine called *Muscat-de-Beni-Amar*.

TUNISIA

The first wine was made in Tunisia by the Carthaginians, but this was not wine as we know it, since it was made with raisins. At this period the Tunisians had, for the time, quite a flourishing export trade. Subsequently the country came under the domination of the Muslims, so naturally, all consumption of alcohol became taboo. As a result, all knowledge of wine making was lost without trace and the revival of vinous knowledge is really very recent indeed. In any event it is little likely that the wine-producing scope of this country will ever be in any way comparable to that of neighbouring Algeria, as the rainfall is extremely slight and the heat tremendous – far too intense for the cultivation of the vine except along the coastal strips.

Production in Tunisia really began when the phylloxera disease ravaged European vineyards. There were in Tunisia at this time many French and Italian migrants (neither have ever been backward in coming forward when it is a matter of profit making!) and they immediately seized the obvious opportunity, planted vines and prospered considerably. As a result of the ravages made by the dread phylloxera, high prices were being paid for any table wines.

By 1910 there were over forty thousand acres in cultivation, but it was not until after the First World War that it really got under way. By this time the number of European settlers had escalated, mainly due to help given by the French Government to war veterans. This took the form of offering them plots of land and loans for the purchase of vines and equipment – an admirable attempt to encourage the growth of wine. By 1933 there were around 172,000 acres under cultivation. Regrettably the result of this rapid development was the production of a large quantity of low-grade wine whose chief feature, at that time, was that of high alcoholic strength and as such it was seized on as a blending agent by the French for their wines.

Then the French Government introduced a quota system for the import into France of this wine and so, almost immediately, a great deal of acreage was taken out of cultivation. This was when the Tunisians decided to concentrate on quality instead of quantity; they forbade the addition of sugar; they forbade the sale of thin wines; the whole trade became rigidly controlled, as it still is by the Tunisian Government. Permission has to be obtained for every new planting and for the entire process of production to be set in train.

The main wine areas are at Cap Bon, Tunis, Grumbellia, Bizerta, Taboulba and Mateur. Red, rosé and both dry and sweet white wines of very reasonable quality are now being produced and sold at highly competitive prices. I have recently sampled a selection of these wines which can be obtained easily in Tunisia and which the producers hope to sell in this country.

Carthage Rosé is very dry, fruity and rather flinty. Served well chilled, as all their rosés and whites should be, I found it extremely pleasant.

Koudiat Rosé is a fairly dry wine up to the standard of some of the better Provençal wines. My wife and I drank quite a lot of it when we were in Tunisia.

Koudiat white was also our favourite dry white and well above the average.

Koudiat red is deep in colour, has very little nose, but it does have a certain distinction and is rather full-bodied.

Tyna is a dark red, sturdy wine with quite a reasonable bouquet when mature. I sampled a 1964 and found it had a very slight resemblance to a young Burgundy.

Haut Mornag is a fairly deep-coloured rosé – not as dry as the others. It would appeal, I think, to many palates as an *Amontillado* Sherry does in competition with a *Fino*.

Sidi Raise Rosé is really a brown wine like a much deeper version of France's *Pelure d'Oignon*. It is medium dry and fairly heavy.

ALGERIA

The wine industry of Algeria only came into existence in 1830 when the French captured the country and, as in the other North African countries, French settlers started to come over. Land could be obtained for practically nothing and labour was also very cheap, so most of them planted vineyards. Again the coastal strip was the only suitable location for vine growing and the first vineyards were planted around Algiers. However, more practical sites were soon discovered west of Algiers in the Oran département and more still were started near Constantine. Eventually over half the vineyards were in the Oran region, about a quarter round Algiers and about the same near Constantine. The fertile coastal plain produced record quantities of wine but it was practically all of a fairly low quality. By 1880 the yield was up to about nine and a half million gallons. This was the time when phylloxera had devastated the French vineyards so the Algerians were able to obtain very high prices for their products, thus they planted an increasing acreage and continued so to do for over seventy years. By this time the French had re-planted their vineyards with new stock grafted on to disease-resisting American roots and the enormous production of Algerian wine was soon in excess of the demand.

In the late 1950s came the long and very costly civil war and after four years the Muslims were victorious, so the majority of the French residents, many born in the country, as were their parents and grand-parents, fled. Over thirty thousand vineyards which they had begun and run were appropriated by the new native administration and sold to the highest bidder.

The wines produced by the French settlers were still red, white and rosé, mostly of the *ordinaire* type, but there were a few of good quality. The reds were dark in colour and full-bodied and as they had a high alcoholic strength the French again bought tremendous quantities to blend with their much lighter wines.

While it is generally accepted that Algerian wines come into the category of 'plonk', under the French domination of Algeria this was not wholly true; I was told frequently when as a young man I lived in France that Frenchmen kept extremely quiet about Algerian wines. They were bargains of a kind to the French wine industry, which would have suffered a very severe setback without them.

THE WINES OF
SOUTH AMERICA

In dealing with the lower-priced wines we cannot ignore those imported from South America. Even so, we need only concern ourselves with two countries therein – Chile and the Argentine.

CHILE

The wine industry of Chile only started seriously in the middle of the nineteenth century or, to be absolutely accurate, in 1851 when French experts were invited to the country. They brought with them a large number of good French vines and instructed painstakingly on their planting and cultivation. Even so, the majority of the vineyards are small even today, but there are now over thirty-two thousand of them altogether.

The Chilean Government, when not fully occupied with revolutions, attaches great importance to wine, as indeed they should do, and not only do they help the growers with loans but they have actually got around to making laws controlling not only the quality and composition of the wines but also the precise amount of acreage. It is unfortunate and tragic to have to add that Chile is one of the few wine-producing countries which suffers from a high degree of alcoholism through wine drinking!

My first experience of Chilean wines was some years ago. They were then unknown in this county and it was so unfortunate an experience that it was a long time before I could be persuaded to sample Chilean wines again. It came about, when I was visiting an Australian friend who owned a restaurant in the West End of London. We settled down to a pleasant evening of gossip. All went well until he introduced his latest discovery – Chilean red wine. Again unfortunately, we all imbibed rather too freely of what was in fact a rough, very strong and heavy beverage and I regret to have to confess that I was far from my best and freshest next day. That is the difference between drinking a low-quality wine and a really good one. The latter leaves no after-effects.

However, since that time, either the quality of the wine has improved considerably or we are importing better Chilean wines, for there are several very palatable red ones available over here now. There are basically three kinds produced in Chile, rich ones, including some in the north which are fortified, good-quality dry red and white ones in the centre and some remarkably undistinguished ones in the south.

Chile is one of the few countries which has never suffered from an attack upon its vines by the dreaded phylloxera. This, so it is said, is due to the protection from the Andes and the Pacific Ocean. This means that the stocks grow on their own roots and do not have to be grafted on to resistant stock.

In the north the vineyards are found between the Choapa river and the Atacama desert and the wines here have an extremely high alcoholic content. The majority of the production is distilled and made into Brandy called *Pisco* – to be imbibed with great caution by the uninitiated.

The best wines come from the region of the Maipo Valley, the reds being far and away better than the whites. The former have a good bouquet, are deep red in colour, well balanced and mature well.

ARGENTINA

Whereas the Chilean wine industry derives from French influence, that of Argentina stems from the fact that a large number of Italians settled there at the end of the nineteenth century, and again after the Second World War. There is a very large production, the quantity comparing with that of Algeria which rates fourth in the world. Indeed it attains something in the region of four hundred thousand gallons *per annum*.

Although the bulk is drunk as a daily beverage by the workers there is, even so, an appreciable amount of good-quality wine produced with great care. The dry white wines, like those of Chile, have a lot less character and quality than the reds. While quite a few of these are produced from a single type of grape, the majority are the result of the blending not only of several types of grape but of the wine of several years. The results are very palatable and they are resonably priced. The ordinary reds are often matured for about three years but the whites are drunk very young.

Argentinians also make a number of sparkling wines, usually sweet and of no great account, plus a quantity of fortified wines of the Port and Sherry type, quite unremarkable to nose, palate and taste-buds.

The main wine-producing area is the Mendoza region with the San Juan district coming a good second.

Of the South American wines which are currently available over here I would suggest you try: *Chilean Cabernet Reservado* and *Chilean Peteroa Reservado*.

COMMONWEALTH WINES

AUSTRALIA

In any young country the wine industry must obviously be young too – at least by European standards. In fact, the first Australian vines were planted at Parramatta in 1788 by a Captain Arthur Philip, the first Governor of the Colony of New South Wales. They were transported from the Cape of Good Hope and Rio de Janeiro; they somehow managed to survive this journey and, after much initial experimenting, established themselves in good health. Then in 1816 the explorer Gregory Blaxland planted a vineyeard and from the grapes produced a red wine of his own. Four years later the first commercial vineyard was planted by John MacArthur, the pioneer of the Australian Merino sheep industry. He had first made, like the wise man he was, an extensive journey through France and Switzerland in order to study viticulture; by 1827 he was producing around twenty thousand gallons of wine annually.

In 1830 a young Scot, James Busby, planted a vineyard in Hunter Valley in New South Wales, which is one of the main wine centres today. By 1852 he was producing sixty thousand gallons of wine annually, plus a thousand gallons of Brandy. These wines range from light table ones to sweet dessert types.

Then in 1834 the colony of Victoria was founded and wine planting went on apace. When the Murray river was developed through a huge reservoir being attached, this part of the country – called Mildura – became by far the most important area of Victoria. The

E

grapes flourished and produced large quantities of the Sherry- and Port-type pressings.

In spite of the start these two colonies had, South Australia – made an independent state in 1838 – soon overtook them; owing to good rainfall and warm summers tempered by the sea breezes, this area rapidly became the most important centre of the wine industry, a position which it has retained to this day.

The most productive area of South Australia is the Barossa Valley, where the vines are protected by dense afforestation on the hillsides. The vines grow on the gentler slopes and in the wide, well-drained valley. Every year an enormous vintage festival is held which has become one of the gayest of all the Australian festivals. One can speculate as to whether or not this gaiety is due to the ancestry of the people concerned, who, after all, came to these Australian vineyards from all over Europe; indeed, many of their European customs persist hereabouts to this day. The wine production runs a gamut from the lightest to the very full-bodied.

A small quantity of fine wine comes from Western Australia and a little from Queensland.

Being such a vast continent, Australian climatic conditions range from the tropical in the north to the very cold – with snow on the mountains – in the south. So, obviously, it was comparatively easy to find ideal situations for wine production. These areas are warmer and drier than in Europe. They have an adequate rainfall in the winter and hot, dry sunny conditions in the summer, and there are no great variations from year to year. These conditions, combined with the fact that a tremendous amount of blending is employed, ensure a constant standard. The only real snag is that the climate is almost too good! This results in a very high sugar concentration and therefore the majority of wines are very full-bodied indeed. The reds average three per cent more alcohol than any similar European wines.

All the white wines are drunk very young as are most of the reds, rather in the same way as *Beaujolais*. They like to breathe much more than European reds, so the Australians (who should know!) recommend that the corks be drawn from three to seven hours before consumption.

The bulk of the table wines are named after their European counterparts, like *Burgundy, Claret* and *Chablis,* or after the grape variety such as *Riesling*; do not, but, commit the cardinal error of judging them against their namesakes, for they all have their own very particular characteristics and in no way resemble the Europeans whose names they bear.

SOUTH AFRICA

South African wine growing has a fairly long history. In 1652 Jan Van Riebeeck – the Cape Colony's founder – landed with a small band of traders and Dutch East India Company's employees. He spent the ensuing ten years in building up a seal fishery, but during this period he also planted his first vines. These flourished; so much so that four years later he produced and declared his first vintage.

Gradually more of the settlers followed suit and began to produce quite drinkable but really very ordinary wines. There was one exception, a man called Simon Van Der Stel, who on his own estate at Groot Constantia began turning out what was unquestionably the best wine in the colony.

This state of affairs might have lasted a very long time but for one of those extraordinary acts of timing which never fail to fascinate me. It came about during the reign of Louis XIV of France that the religious differences which arose became the prime cause of Huguenot emigration. Some two hundred or more Huguenots arrived in South Africa and gradually drifted south to the Cape. They brought with them the great technical knowledge of France, plus, of course, a real appreciation of good wine. They found in the Cape a perfect wine-growing climate with plenty of rain in the winter, uninterrupted sunshine in the summer and the heat nicely tempered by the trade winds, plus the inestimable bonus of virtually no rainfall during the critical, ripening period of autumn.

For a long time, however, there was only one really outstanding wine – the aforementioned *Constantia* – Van Der Stel's sweet white wine. Then the British took over the colony in 1795 and when the Napoleonic Wars cut off all supplies of European wines from Britain the Cape wines had their big chance. In 1813 a substantial duty preference was granted by the British Government and by 1824 over a million gallons a year were being exported.

In due course the war ended; although by that time fine vintages were following each other regularly, the preference was gradually reduced as France resumed vinous operations. This resulted in over-production by the South Africans, who found suddenly that they were unable to compete with the newly restored and again flourishing European countries. This state of affairs persisted until exports practically ceased altogether. Eventually wines were selling for as little as a penny a bottle!

Then after the First World War the farmers got together and formed the Co-operative Wine Growers' Association, known as K.W.V. In 1925 Imperial Preference was reintroduced and this was the beginning of the modern Cape wine development which has since shot ahead. Today very large quantities of very good quality wine are exported all over the world.

Unlike a number of other countries the South Africans have not named their wines after their European counterparts but have given them brand names. Some of their wines are identified on their labels by the grape variety's name; others show a particular style like 'Late Vintage' or 'Sparkling'.

The whole wine industry is concentrated in a comparatively small area in the south-east corner of the country, but this countryside is so varied that a large variety of wines can be produced. These range from dry white table wines to full-bodied reds, and include both white and red sweet dessert wines, plus full ranges of fortified wines of the Port and Sherry type.

The dry white wines come mainly from the Paarl, Stellenbosch and Tulbagh districts. The heavier sweeter wines are produced around Worcester, Robertson and Montagu where the *Muscatel* wines and the Brandies are also produced; while the Port types come from Paarl and Stellenbosch. Of them all I would single the following as meriting your special attention, the three most popular table wines available in this country: *Roodeberg* a full-bodied red, *R.W.V. Steen* a dry white, and *K.W.V. Late Vintage* (Steen) medium sweet white.

PORT

Port is frequently called 'the Englishman's Wine' – even in its region of origin, the Douro in the north of Portugal. Here some of the most famous names are British and the creak of the ungreased wooden cart-wheels is often punctuated by the sound of English voices in the vineyard slopes. These run down from the English *quintas* to the river Douro whence, in the past – but alas no longer – the barrels were carried downstream to Oporto. There is a lot of 'alas' about Port. Only a few remote, surviving vineyards still 'tread' the grapes in the old traditional manner, but I am happy to say that I have shared in those traditional vintage rituals when the barefoot men link arms and, standing in the *largars* or tanks, tread the grapes all through the nights singing their traditional songs and consuming considerable quantities of *Aguardente*. *Aguardente* survives! It is bar none the producer of the most vicious, protracted hangover of my entire experience.

A still further 'alas' derives from the traditional service of Port, from decanters, with dessert nuts and salt, as the climax to a fine dinner and after all the 'covers' have been drawn. Then the decanter is 'launched' by the host, and sent clockwise round the table, passed from hand to hand, each guest serving himself and then 'passing the Port'. Woe betide the man who failed to follow this ritual of 'passing', which would inevitably evoke a courteous but sub-acid comment from the host: 'Henry, I believe the Port is with you, dear boy!'

None of this is necessary and the 'alas' *leit motif* lies in the fact that none of this (to me charming and traditional) ritual is of the slightest importance for the simple enjoyment of a good glass of port.

Firstly, there is no need to decant – save where the Port is vintage and of an age to cause a sediment in the base of the bottle. As the price of such Ports is positively prohibitive today, they have no place in a modest book about wines for all of us, they are of no consequence to us and we can forget all about them.

Here let me stress that Port is a generic and not a specific title and that Port can be enjoyed, just as you and I enjoy a glass of Sherry, before a meal, with certain dishes during a meal and at the end of a meal, either with fruit and or nuts or with a mouthful of honest cheese. This is not to play ostrich in respect of the ultimate cheese – the magnificence of, say, French Roquefort as a dream partner to a glass of good Tawny or, if you win the Pools, Vintage Port – but again, price is the dominant factor and the cost of French cheeses as against our own good British ones puts them out of court too in a book of this kind.

While mentioning the French, may I draw your attention to the plain fact that the Centre of the Gastronomic World – France – lags far behind 'perfidious Albion' in the matter of Port appreciation. In this context I still shudder at the recollection of spending Christmas in a Normandy farmhouse with my Paris manager's family. On Christmas morning the men of the farmhouse party hurried to a village rendezvous where we were all regaled with sweet Ruby Port and chocolates before, as I knew only too well, returning to a feast which would have scared the pants off Gargantua. Even so, I must stick to my guns even regarding this, to me, horrific experience – that the wine you like is the right wine for you and a fig for all those pompous 'experts'!

I have deliberately cited this example in an effort to fight my prime 'alas' concerning Port – that many people have been scared right off attempting to drink Port because of all the panoply of chi-chi with which it has been invested.

Despite everything, it is nevertheless reassuring to find that the sales of Port in Britain rose by twenty-five per cent in 1972; by a further ten per cent in 1973 and are still rising. Please note that these sales, understandably, are low on Vintage Ports but, of the remainder around sixty per cent are of Ruby Port and forty per cent of Tawny Port.

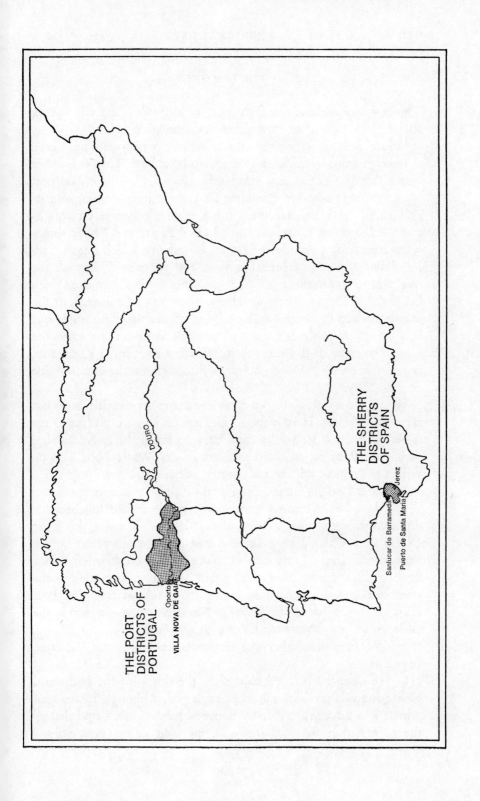

THE PORT
DISTRICTS OF
PORTUGAL

DOURO

Oporto
VILLA NOVA DE GAIA

THE SHERRY
DISTRICTS
OF SPAIN

Sanlucar de Barrameda
Jerez
Puerto de Santa Maria

WHITE PORT

This is where we examine Port types and see when and where they fit into our pattern of eating and drinking pleasure.

White Port is, classically, the only one which can be served correctly as an aperitif. It should always be chilled. Then it is either drunk 'straight' from any small tulip-shaped glass or classic port glass, or else it is served Portuguese style as a long, cooling, thirst-quenching drink in a tall glass. It is known affectionately throughout the Douro as 'breakfast wine'. Indeed Fanny and I have somewhat strenuous memories of Douro hospitality which began with ice-clinking glasses of breakfast wine and progressed through the day with Ports various in large quantities until it climaxed with '22 and '27 Vintage Ports at dinner. Fanny and I learned – in the matter of lace-up shoes – to kick these off and likewise insert our feet into them without having to bend down to tie and untie the laces. The cause of this eccentricity, which we regard as a necessity, *spots before the eyes*! Douro hospitality does err on the extreme side of generosity.

We do, however, serve ourselves and many guests with 'breakfast wine' in summer. Here is the recipe, in case you would like to try it for yourselves. Half fill a tumbler with crushed ice. Add a slice of lemon. Pour on a double measure of dry White Port. Top up with a generous squirt of soda water, stir and sip.

All other Ports, Vintage, Tawny and Ruby, are dessert wines and should be served at room temperature at the end of luncheon or dinner. Incidentally, regarding the 'circulating' clockwise, this is the British way which I have already explained, but there is also the Portuguese variant – that men serve the women on their left before sending the decanter on its way again. If you wish to stick to the traditional service then there is one hard-and-fast rule that Port must never be passed backwards. Nor may it yo-yo across the table as to my horror was done in the *Forsyte Saga* on British television. Pray remember that this series was set in the Victorian hey-day!

I have often been asked to explain the origin of the traditional circulation of Port in the manner explained. Although I have read what a great many accepted 'authorities' have to say, I find that all the expressed reasons disagree and, speaking purely personally, I think Mr Rupert Croft-Cooke's is the most practical, if unromantic, explanation. Mr Croft-Cooke says – I quote – 'If a man has filled the glass on his own right-hand side, the only way in which he can set it (bottle or decanter) beside his neighbour's glass without stretching across anyone is by handing it to the man on his left.' The only snag here is that if there is no other more picturesque explanation why is Port not served in the same way as any table wine?

As to smoking, the rule stems from the Factory House in Oporto. This is the mundane name given to the splendid club which was formed in the eighteenth century by the leading Port men of the period. Dinners are celebrations of such splendour that both my wife and I count ourselves immensely privileged in having been invited to share in them. Here then is the ruling of the greatest 'Port Experts'. When Vintage Port is being circulated, cigars and cigarettes are proffered, for the first time *after* the Port has completed its first circuit and returned to the host. When Tawny Port is being circulated Port, cigars and cigarettes are launched simultaneously; once again I stress that if you think this is all a lot of unnecessary nonsense and fuss pray stick to your guns. The great affair is to drink Ports and enjoy them after your own fashion. Whatever seems to you the most agreeable and comfortable way must be right and proper for you and never more emphatically so than in the enjoyment of 'The Englishman's Wine'.

A SHORT HISTORY OF PORT

This is a solemn vinous subject and it would be terrible for me and for all wine lovers among you if we did not accord it proper respect and therefore I am giving you a brief résumé of its history.

Port is fortified wine grown in the upper Douro mountains in northern Portugal within the confines of a strictly defined area. When the wine has been made it is transferred to the great wine lodges of Vila Nova de Gaia, which is an enclosed and closely guarded suburb of Oporto. Types range from the greatest *Vintage Port*, through *Crusted Port* (Ruby), to *Wooded Port* (Tawny) and down to *White Port* (Dry).

After the fall of the old Roman Empire great vintage wines disappeared and it was left to the Portuguese, fifteen centuries later, to rediscover the lost secret that fine wine would mature in glass to a

glorious old age just as it had done in the airtight earthenware jars
of Roman usage and for conservation.

Portuguese wine has been imported into England since the earliest
Anglo-Portuguese Treaty. This was first signed in 1353 in
London. The widespread use of Port in Britain is generally agreed
to date from the Methuen Treaty of 1703. This treaty guaranteed
a tariff preference for Portuguese wines over French wines; it also
gave security to shippers and growers which encouraged them to
make the long series of experiments which ultimately gave us the
peerless Ports of today. The locally grown wine called *Consumo* was
heavy and harsh, with all the sugar converted into alcohol through
fermenting in a hot climate. Alas, with these depressing qualities
Consumo could not compete with other countries' table wines,
even with the preferential terms awarded by the treaty so something
had to be done. The goal was the checking of fermentation
while leaving a reasonable proportion of the natural sugar in the
wine.

By the process of trial and error it was eventually discovered that
the addition of Brandy produced the required result. Unfortunately
this led to tremendous arguments for it shocked the purists to the
core. They maintained that any interference with the natural course
of fermentation was a sacrilege! It was many years before it became
generally accepted that the addition of Brandy was not only a vast
improvement but transformed the wine into one of unparalleled
quality. The late M. André L. Simon said that 'Great Claret might be
called a masterpiece of nature; great Port a masterpiece of man'.
It has been increasingly cherished, cosseted and protected down the
years. In 1756 the Douro Wine Company was formed under Royal
Charter and there is no doubt that although there were many abuses
of its principles it exerted a powerful influence. Its main decrees
were:

1. A definition of the boundaries where the Port character wines
   could be grown.
2. It appointed tasters to classify the Douro wines as fit for export
   or not.
3. No elderberries were to be used to deepen the colour, a
   pernicious practice which had the effect of dulling the delicate
   flavour of the wine.

Since then many safeguards of quality have been introduced, culminating in 1932 when the Portuguese Government set up three bodies to control the growing, making and export of Port – the Port Wine Institute, working with the Port Wine Shippers' Guild in charge of all exports of the Douro House which supervises the farms and vineyards. The Institute has full powers to inspect all wine lodges; it also grants the certificates of origin or export licences, but only after its own highly experienced and skilful tasters have passed the wine. These first few outlines will serve to confirm the rightness of my 'Simon' quote – that Port is, in fact, 'a masterpiece of man'.

By the beginning of the nineteenth century Vintage Port had proved itself to be the finest of all dessert wines. It has remained so ever since. The first great known vintage is that of 1775, by which time the glass bottle was in use, although it was still not known how it could be used to best advantage. The first recorded vintage was that of 1797, but there are many conflicting opinions about its quality and, indeed, at this point it would be a good idea if we tackled the somewhat vital question, 'What is Vintage Port?'

It is, in fact, the best of all Ports, possibly ten per cent of a single, exceptionally good year. Usually it is the blending of wines from several vineyards, but sometimes the wine of a single *quinta* (wine-growing estate) which is kept in barrels for two years and then either bottled in Oporto, or more usually in the country to which it is exported. Britain is easily the largest buyer of such wine. The selected Port then has to remain in bottle for at least twenty years before it is considered to be fully matured. Nowadays, there is a consensus of opinion taken on when to declare a vintage year, but this is not a uniform decision. At times only a few houses may consider their wine worthy of this distinction, while many more will include themselves out!

While the Douro has established its reputation with these very fine wines, it is obviously not economically practical to concentrate wholly upon them since they are, in any case, only available in exceptional years and also because their cost puts them beyond the pocket of the average consumer; other means of production had to be found to dispose of the great grape harvest and the final outcome of many more experiments became *Tawny Port*. This is a blend of the wine of several years left in the wood for ten to fifteen years until it has faded to the colour that its name implies – Ports age much faster in the barrel than in the bottle. A really good, old Tawny is probably the best Port of all for many palates, as it has a wonderful bouquet and, being somewhat lighter than Vintage Port, is smoother and a little drier on the palate.

Next in line comes *Ruby Port* which is also matured in wood. This is bottled and marketed much earlier than Tawny and before the colour changes. It is therefore not so mature and consequently it sells at a lower price.

In the Vintage Port category there is also *Crusted Port*, which is a blend of several years, left in the barrel for a little longer than Vintage Port before being bottled. This matures in seven to eight years, throwing a heavy crust – hence the name!

A Port that is becoming more and more popular nowadays is *Late Bottled Vintage*. This is bottled after six to ten years in the wood, by which time the deposit has sunk to the bottom of the barrel and the bottled wine is clear. It is ready for drinking very soon after bottling and although rather lighter than true Vintage Port nevertheless makes an excellent drink.

Finally, there is *White Port*, which is made by the same process as Red Port, but from white grapes instead of black and with fermentation stopped much later, so that it is considerably drier and makes a splendid aperitif wine.

THE MAKING OF PORT

The vineyards of the Douro are remarkable, and remarkably different from those of any other wine growers. They are terraced. They were constructed at enormous effort actually on the steep hillside, where they sweep up to the skyline in tier upon tier. The very best Port wine grapes come from the vines on the middle slopes or tiers. It is a wonderful sight when the vines are in full leaf to see these rows upon rows of terraces rising up from the great valleys with, far below them, the river Douro which Fanny has always likened to Mr Rudyard Kipling's 'great grey-green, greasy Limpopo River'.

At vintage time the pickers come from many miles round to pick vineyard by vineyard in a carefully planned rotation. Each vineyard manager has buildings for these men and women where they are housed and fed during their stays. They invariably travel in large groups, tramping along to the lilting music of their own small bands. These people are tough and whenever they stop to quench their thirst they 'relax their muscles' by dancing on the terrain which is really only suited to mountain goats!

On arrival at each vineyard they set to work exactly as their ancestors did before them. The women cut the grape bunches with knives and scissors, and then remove any defective ones before heaping the clusters into small baskets. These are then transferred to enormous baskets, each holding up to one hundred and thirty pounds of grapes. These baskets are then hoisted on to the men's backs, where they are balanced by a leather support which hangs down between the shoulder blades and is suspended from a broad leather band fastened across the forehead. Thus laden, the bearers hop down the terraces, usually barefooted, and jump down from one wall to another – sometimes from a height of up to fifteen feet. On arrival at the *adegas* (storehouses) they shoot the grapes into the *largar* (a large stone tank) and promptly return for another load. So tough are they that except for meal breaks they can keep this up from soon after dawn until sunset, after which they spend the evenings singing and dancing in the halls put at their disposal by the vineyards' owners. When their comparatively brief sleep period comes round you will hear the rhythm of their indefatigable musicians rising up strongly as the procession winds past the *quinta* towards the sleeping quarters; soon after first light it all begins again as the little bands play everyone back to another laughter-filled day of gruelling labour under a blazing sun.

Regrettably, from this stage onwards the old colourful method has practically disappeared, as I have already said.

Now the grapes are fed straight into machines which crush them and remove the stalks. Then the juices are pumped into enormous vats and the 'must', or newly pressed grape juice, is kept cool until the vat is full in order to hold back the beginning of the fermentation. Only when the temperature is stepped up does the fermentation begin; it is then allowed to continue for several days. The critical moment comes after this when the manager must decide on the exact time to stop the fermentation. This is done by running off the wine into large casks and adding Brandy to it. There it remains for the winter and when spring comes it is transported in the casks down to the wine lodges of Vila Nova de Gaia. Here all the blending is done and the final wine is left in barrel for two years for Vintage Port and up to thirty years for very old Tawny.

One of the old customs still extant at vintage time is the nightly dancing, to which I have already made a passing reference. Drinks are provided by the 'house' and the manager and his assistants move round giving out cigars and cigarettes and also dancing with the workers. It is a charming and slightly feudal ritual. When dinner is over in the *quinta* the house party moves down and if they entertain any notions of grandeur on arrival, half an hour is enough to bring them down to size as they are caught up in the stamping, whirling, shouting mêlée, while the thumping feet raise small duststorms from the hard soil flooring.

THE HISTORY OF THE FACTORY HOUSE

The Factory House stands as a memorial to the great partnership between the British and Portuguese who have worked together in great amity throughout many centuries. The name is terrible, since it has, in fact, nothing whatsoever to do with a factory; originally it was called *The Factors House*. It is such an exclusive club that only the British Port shippers are members. The money for it was raised through the Contributions Fund Act which levied a special tax on goods exported from Oporto in British ships. The foundations were laid in 1785 and it was completed by 1790.

Unlike the great, ornate palaces built in Venice and Genoa by the Italian merchant princes, the British merchants of Oporto contented themselves with a plain, austere exterior of Portuguese granite and of Georgian architectural design, which depends entirely upon its splendid proportions for its distinction. It makes an odd contrast to all the encircling, over-elaborate Portuguese buildings.

When you cross the threshold into the cool, columned vestibule you will notice the curious arched spaces, each of just sufficient size to take a sedan-chair. In fact, one such chair still exists there, the sole survivor of what was probably the earliest 'parking', when the 'Link Men' parked their chairs in the now empty bays. The great staircase of granite slabs is illuminated by small lamps on long rods; these were used by the chair-bearers, they are now (another alas!) electric.

There is a nostalgically beautiful ballroom hung with superb chandeliers and it is fascinating to stand there and reflect upon what this ballroom must have looked like when the thousands of sconces were filled with candles and the light from them sparkled on the elaborate uniforms of Wellington's victorious officers and on the jewels of the women with whom they danced.

There is a most impressive library too and a pair of dining saloons. When you dine in these great rooms you do so off a 'service' of Coalport which can serve over a hundred 'covers'. It made the journey from England by sea during the eighteenth century.

The dining ritual on formal occasions is the most fantastic part of this remarkable club. The two identical dining rooms are divided by the folding mahogany doors which are closed during the service of the many courses. Guests dine at an enormous D-ended Sheraton dining table. Then as dinner moves towards the climax – the Port stage – these giant doors are folded back. The diners rise, turn so that all face towards these doors and then move straight into the second dining room and resume their seating precisely as before. Here, at the uncovered replica mahogany table with its crystal decanters in their Georgian coasters, a great crystal bowl of dark red roses as a centrepiece and pyramids of dessert set down the centre of the table left and right of the rosebowl, the Port is served! All this is done so that there is no fear that the smell of the food would contaminate the precious Port, which is then launched upon its first circuit by the host.

SHERRY

The great wine of Spain is Sherry, the most popular of all fortified wines in England – we take eighty per cent of the entire exports. It is made by the *Solera* system, as you will see later on, and therefore never dated. Sherry, like Port, is a fortified wine, which means that alcohol is added to it at some stage in the making. It is also a blended wine and gains in alcoholic strength as it ages in wood. It is one of the most versatile wines in the world, varying from very pale dry to very rich indeed. In fact it is a wine for all occasions. If you dine in a restaurant in Jerez you will be given Sherry to drink throughout the meal and, surprising enough, it is so sturdy that it can even stand tobacco.

The word Sherry is a corruption of *Xerex*, the original name for the town now called Jerez. In Spain the name can only be applied to wines made within the triangle framed by Jerez, Puerto de Santa Maria and Sanlucar de Barrameda, and it is shipped from the port of Cadiz, which is only twenty miles away from 'the triangle'. It is a great pity that the Spaniards have never been able to prevent the name being used in other countries, because as matters stand the Australians sell wine they call 'Sherry', so do the South Africans, the Cypriots and others, all of which may be excellent wines in their own way, but are not Sherry.

Although, as in most of the wine-producing countries, modernization has ousted the traditional methods of collecting and pressing in some vineyards, nevertheless there is much of the old colourful way left. The harvesters come from miles around and are usually housed and fed. They use knives, not small shears, to cut the grape bunches and have baskets which they fill and then tie on small, straw head pads to balance the baskets and keep them steady with one hand. The grapes are conveyed to a central collecting point where the rotten or dried-up grapes (*sequillas*) are removed and the remaining fruit is then carried on donkeys to the yard outside the main building (*almijar*). In this yard the bunches are laid on to small round grass mats and left for twelve hours or more to dry out in the sun, so that they are quite dry when they reach the wine presses (*lagares*). These *lagares* are wooden troughs roughly ten feet square and sloped from back to front to allow the juice to run down to a spout, from whence it runs into a vat and is poured into barrels. In the middle of the *lagar* stands the hand press.

Also in each *lagar* there are several men stripped to shorts and a shirt and, unlike Madeira where they are barefooted, they wear boots with special studs. Each man is issued with a wooden spade.

The treading is done at night and they go on treading hour after hour apparently tirelessly and work from back to front shovelling back the trodden grapes as they go – all this is done to a special rhythm. Next the *marc* (the skin, pips and stalks) is pushed into the press and tied and bound up. The wooden lid is put on and held in place by a special nut with handles about three feet long. The screw is then turned and gradually tightened until all the juice has been extracted.

The filled butts are then conveyed to the storage house (*bodega*) which is beautifully cool and here the fermentation commences. At first it is fermented very fast and then the process is slowed down. Before it is 'racked' (drawn off into barrels) alcohol is first added to these barrels. The *Solera* system used is simple. The wine is transferred, after the alcohol process, into butts. These are then, more often than not, stacked so that the oldest is at the base and the youngest at the top. At the appropriate time, half or two-thirds, but never more, of wine for bottling is drawn from the bottom or oldest butts and these butts are then filled up again, the oldest from the next oldest and so on to the youngset. This process goes on *ad infinitum*.

The two main categories of Sherry are *Finos*, pale and dry, and *Olorosos*, darker and sweeter. In the *Fino* group the driest is *Manzanilla*, which has characteristics all of its own; it comes from the Sanlucar de Barrameda district by the sea, which gives it the distinctive, clean, but slightly bitter taste and it is a fact that it must be drunk *in situ* if you wish to enjoy this distinctive flavour to the full. It simply does not travel well and even when transported to Jerez, only a few miles away, it loses its distinction fast and becomes an ordinary *Fino*. Conversely a wine from Jerez grapes when taken to Sanlucar will assume the character of *Manzanilla*.

Also in the *Fino* group is the *Palma* type. This is a pale, dry Sherry, but it is never as dry as the *Manzanillas*. It comes from either Jerez or Puerto de Santa Maria and, although still comparatively little known in this country, is nevertheless becoming much more popular. It usually carries an additional numerical definition on its labels. Therefore you may expect to find *Palmas Una* (meaning first group), *Palmas Dos* (second group), *Palmas Tres* (third group) and *Palmas Cuatro* (fourth group); just to make things more confusing the Spaniards put number one at the bottom and number four at the top, which is worth remembering as, instinctively, one thinks of the fourth group as being three degrees lower than the first. By their nature these are automatically aperitif Sherries, whereas, as we shall see later, there are some very rich ones which can also become what are called dessert types. For an example – let me suggest that one of the few suitable drinks to take with a rich black Christmas pudding is a dessert Sherry – and then deal with it in full when we come to the relevant category.

Under the heading *Fino* we also find *Amontillado*. This is probably the most popular, for, being only medium dry, it is a kind of alcoholic halfway house among these fortified wines, and therefore appeals to people who like a fairly dry Sherry and to those who find the *Manzanillas* and the *Palmas* too dry for their palates. While these *Amontillados* are still pale-coloured wines, they are darker than the other two which I have just mentioned. The name originally derives from the village of Montilla, but nowadays, the Montilla wines are something quite separate; they now no longer qualify as Sherry, having been granted the right in 1944 by the Spanish Government to call themselves just *Montillas*. They are light, dry and delicate and are fast building up a reputation for themselves.

In the second, as it were, parent category we find the *Olorosos* and among them I think we should tackle *Palo Cortado* which in some instances is classified, as I explained for the *Palmas*, with the numbers on the labels rising in a reverse category to our natural thinking, from number one, which is, in fact, the humblest to number four the most elevated. A great number of people fail to realize that *Palo Cortado* is an *Oloroso* and think of it more as a halfway stage between *Finos* and other *Olorosos*. This confusion arises because the taste is very similar to that of the *Amontillados* although these Sherries do have the extra body characteristics of *Olorosos*. I know this is somewhat confusing but I hope I have made it clear.

At this juncture, and before I define any other Sherries whatsoever, I must make the point that in Spain, which is the country of origin, all Sherries are dry. These are generally referred to as natural Sherries. As a generalization, a great many of them are far too dry for the average English palate and therefore they are doctored, not in any derogatory sense, but merely so treated that their dryness is diminished before importation to these shores. It must be remembered that all the sugar content in the grape turns into alcohol in the process of fermentation and therefore Sherry has no natural sweetness at all. So the doctoring is done by the addition of small quantities of a sweetening wine made from a grape called *Pedro Ximenez*.

These grapes are dried in the sun for anything from twelve to twenty days. This greatly reduces the quantity of liquid and of course makes it too expensive to use for anything but blending in small amounts.

There is in fact a classification very little used in Spain, but very familiar to English shippers. It is called *Amorosos*, a term which signifies exactly what I have just explained, that the Sherries so labelled have been sweetened.

Thus we come to Milk, Cream and Brown Sherries, all of which have been so sweetened by wine made from sun-dried grapes and this is how we arrive at the dessert Sherries to which I referred a few paragraphs ago. These are dessert wines; they are frequently offered as an alternative to Port with dessert, but unlike Port they are not suitable, as Port is, above all, to partner cheese.

To sum up I would say that it is very difficult to attempt to udge from a Sherry label exactly what kind of wine is contained in the bottle, for, to add to the confusion of the uninitiated, it is the curious habit of many English importers to classify Sherries by their colour. Thus you will have a very pale or a pale Sherry which could turn out to be a *Manzanilla* or an *Amontillado*. Equally, you could broach a bottle carrying just such a colour label stating golden, amber or brown, which on tasting could turn out to be one of either the *Olorosos, Palo Cortados* or *Amorosos*. Frankly I would say to you that there is only one safe way (a) to discover what you personally like, and (b) to be sure that what you like is in the bottles of your purchase – *taste it*; provided you can arrange to do so at the hospitality of your wine merchant. Surely this can only prove to be a pleasure.

Before I leave this subject I must say a word or two about the wines of other countries and particularly Australia, South Africa and Cyprus. Although they are styled as Sherries, they are not. Regard them as you would a sparkling wine, made by maybe the Champagne method, but you would not class it as Champagne.

There are some very palatable wines of the Sherry type offered, again in many cases made by similar methods, but you should judge them as separate drinks, not compare them with the genuine article; then you may very well find a drink that is not only to your liking but in most instances very inexpensive.

MADEIRA

Even the name 'Madeira' is evocative of vinous history, colourful tradition and elegant ceremony and ritual.

The island is Portuguese, but the men and women who made vinous history and who, until very recently, were the most dominant figures on the island, were British. Their possessions, their vinous knowledge and experience, their *quintas*, all were outstanding and all grew from comparatively modest beginnings. Indeed, one of the greatest figures crossed the Atlantic eight times under sail, married a Blandy, thus attaining the now extinct title of Mistress Blandy. During her very long and colourful life she entertained the leading figures of the world and dispensed great Madeiras to them.

My wife and I had the privilege of some slight experience in this matter. We were bidden on our first visit to take luncheon with the, by this time old and fragile, *grande dame*. We travelled up – all roads go up from Funchal – in a massive old Daimler and were received *en famille*. My wife still declares that when she saw the tiny, white-haired figure of her hostess standing erect at the farther end of about forty feet of parquet she had the greatest difficulty in stopping herself from dropping a curtsey! At the subsequent luncheon, for four persons, taken at a table covered with Mechlin lace, set with silver of the first and second Georges, with a footman behind each chair, our frail hostess apologized for the informality with which we were being received, since she had heard we preferred somewhat informal and intimate occasions.

On another occasion, when dining with Mistress Blandy's son, the late Graham Blandy, then the 'uncrowned King of Madeira', he confided to Fanny when pouring her a glass of very old Madeira, 'You know, Fanny, this *Tarrantez* was in bottle three years before Marie Antoinette was beheaded.' It was perfect and the fitting climax to a memorable meal which commenced with *foie gras* from Strasbourg and went on to roast peacock, taken at a D-ended Sheraton table set in a key design of fresh, red camellias from the trees with which the Blandy drive is bordered.

Madeira is a small island of two hundred and eighty-five square miles, a little larger than the Isle of Wight in fact. It is semi-tropical, mountainous, volcanic and has only one town, Funchal, the capital, where the main avenue is blue in spring with the blossoms of jacaranda trees. There are, of course, a number of little villages besides, notably Camara de Lobos where Sir Winston Churchill used to paint; Camacha where willows are grown for the famous Madeirenses wickerwork, and Machico where João Conçalves (nicknamed 'Zarco') and Tristão Vas Feixeira are said to have landed when they discovered the island in 1419. The island at that time was composed solely of timber and dense vegetation, hence the name Madeira, which in Portuguese means 'wood'. The explorers set fire to the trees to clear a space for a settlement and the blaze is said to have lasted for seven years. This gave the land its particular soil, for the vast accumulation of wood ash increased the fertility so enormously that innumerable varieties of tropical fruits and vegetables and such shrubs and trees as bougainvillaea, orchid, and frangipani immediately began to flourish. This soil was also ideal for grape cultivation and it still imparts to the wine its special smoky flavour.

It was not long before Madeira was colonized, nor before various European grapes were introduced into this distinctive soil. The *Malvoisie* grape was brought from Crete and from it the best known Madeira wine called *Malmsey* was made. The *Verdelho* originated from a cross between the Italian *Verdea* and the Spanish *Pedro Ximenez*, while the *Sercial* wine developed from the German *Riesling*. However, the character of the soil and the climate were instrumental in changing the nature of the wines completely, until over the years they developed their own distinctive characteristics which resulted in the unique wines we can still obtain today.

The British have always exerted tremendous influence over the Madeira wine industry. One of the greater aids to exports in the early days was the edict of Charles II forbidding exports to America and the West Indies of any goods that were not taken in British ships from British ports – but excluding Madeira. So ships passing through invariably took aboard large cargoes of Madeira wines.

Then the English merchants came to the island, so that by 1646, out of twenty-six shippers, no less than ten were British. Many of the old-established families are still in existence, notably the Blandys, the Cossarts, the Leacocks, the Rutherfords, the Mileses and the Henriques.

Shakespeare made frequent references to Madeira, although in Falstaff's day this would have been a browny-red, unfortified wine. A Duke of Clarence, whilst incarcerated in the Tower of London, is reputed to have drowned himself in a barrel of *Malmsey*. The then First Gentleman of Europe, King George IV, had practically nothing else in his Carlton House cellars – at what cost to his liver history does not relate.

So Madeira boomed, but tragedy lay ahead. In 1852 the vines were attacked by a terrible mildew disease called *Oidium Tuckeri* and a considerable period elapsed before it was found that the vines so infected could be cured with sulphur. In all it took nearly ten years for them to recover. By then a number of shippers had left the island and the wine stocks were pathetically depleted, but all was not lost. A few courageous growers set to work to restore their vineyards after this scourge; then in 1872 came fresh disaster. A further scourge that hit Europe, called phylloxera, also appeared on the island and again wiped out all the work of restoration which had been done.

Once more the inhabitants had to start from scratch. Thanks to the efforts of some determined souls, particularly among the English families of that time who had settled there and refused to budge, Madeira wine was restored – not, unfortunately, to its former glory, but still to a very important place in the wine world.

Owing to lack of space (the island being only thirty miles long by sixteen miles wide) and the mountainous nature of the terrain, the grapes are grown high above the ground on trellises which are erected over the very narrow terraces (*estreitos*). At harvest time the pickers are therefore able to reach up and gather the grapes at ease while being protected from the hot sun by the overhead leaves of the growing vines. As in most areas nowadays, practically all the harvest is taken to central points where the grapes are pressed in

modern machines. Only in a very few isolated spots is it still possible
to see the old traditional barefoot treading.

The grapes ripen over a long period due to the varying heights
above sea level of the vineyards so the harvest lasts much longer than
is the case elsewhere. It begins around the end of August with the
Verdelhos and the *Buals* (*Boal* in Portuguese); then progresses to the
Malmseys which have been left to ripen until they are almost as dry
as raisins, and finally to the *Sercials* picked from the highest ground
sometimes late in October.

Some of the presses are situated near the vineyards in outlying
spots, but these are some distance from the lodges where the wine
is made. The newly pressed grapes (*Mosto*) must be moved very
quickly or fermentation will set in. They are mostly transported by
lorry but, like the tradition of barefoot treading, the old method is
still used occasionally. This is by the goatskin carriers (*Borrachieros*);
each man prepares his own skin which is then filled with the *Mosto*,
some ten gallons of it per skin, weighing up to a hundredweight.
Then aided by a sturdy stick the men trudge off with their heavy
loads to the lodges.

Now the fermentation starts, and it is at this stage that the celebrations (*Romarias*) begin. These constitute pilgrimages made to
the holy places on the island where the workers give thanks for the
safe gathering of the grapes. As they are joyful pilgrimages there
is singing and dancing all along the way.

The fermenting of the sweeter wines – the *Buals* and *Malmseys* –
is not allowed to go on for long. It is 'stopped' by the addition of
Brandy. With the drier *Verdelhos* and *Sercials* the fermentation is
permitted to continue for a longer period but this too is checked
from time to time by the addition of small quantities of Brandy. The
wine is then rested for a period before being submitted to a unique
heat process (*Estufagem*). First the wine is transferred into large
Estufa tanks; then it is heated very slowly for some weeks; over this
period the heat is increased gradually to a maximum 122° Fahrenheit.
It is held at this temperature for several weeks and finally the heat
is decreased very slowly until it reaches normal temperature again;
thereafter it is turned into clean vats and allowed to rest in the cool
of the lodges. By law it must not be shipped for a minimum of
thirteen months and this period is usually extended fairly considerably.

Although in the old days there were many 'vintage' Madeiras

it is now only a very exceptional year which yields a vintage wine. Practically all Madeira is blended to obtain uniformity year after year, so, as in Spain for Sherry, the *Solera* system is used. Bear in mind that if you see a bottle labelled 'Solera 1842', the wine of that particular date would form the base only with younger wines 'refreshing' it from year to year, thus instead of being about 130 years old it would have an average age of about seventy years.

This brings us to the subject of grouping. There are four main groups and they are *Sercial, Verdelho, Bual* and *Malmsey.* All are produced from different types of grapes and all are completely different in character too. *Sercial* is the driest. It is a delightful aperitif wine, pale straw to gold in colour, the last to ripen and therefore taking the longest time to mature. Should you encounter a young *Sercial* you will find it very harsh on the palate. For this reason with very rare exceptions, *Sercial* is shipped to us when at least ten to twelve years old. Incidentally with reference to *Sercials* you accept, as generalization, that the paler the wine the drier it is to the palate.

Verdelho is not quite so dry as *Sercial.* It is slightly darker in colour and really does fulfil among Madeiras the function performed by *Amontillados* among Sherries. Both appeal – as moderately dry fortified wines – to palates which reject dry wines. Some of these *Verdelhos* are also dry enough to serve as aperitif wines, but they are at their best when served with *hors-d'œuvre* or melon. You can also serve it with some of those egg dishes which are so very difficult to partner and indeed with some of the more highly flavoured fish dishes.

One of the main virtues of Madeiras is that they are strong enough in character to hold up against any normal food flavour just as they stand up to any climate and to incredibly great age. We must make a clear mental division between these two (*Sercial* and *Verdelho*) and *Bual* and *Malmsey* which are sweet dessert wines with plenty of body and a very fine bouquet, nose or smell. *Bual* makes a splendid marriage with rich puddings. We serve it with that most difficult of all, the traditional black Christmas pudding with which it can, and indeed does, hold its own. It is also the perfect wine companion for rich chocolate puddings like the famous Crème Marie Louise or Ali Bab's Chocolate Cream.

The fourth and greatest of the Madeiras is *Malmsey*; its background is interesting. It originated in the Greek island of Crete where it is called *Malvoisie* and it was brought to Britain by returning Crusaders during the Holy Wars. Eventually the *Malvoisie* grape was introduced to Madeira where it was soon found that the wine produced from it was, by virtue of both the even climate and the fine soil, even better than the original wine produce from Crete.

Malmsey is the sweetest of the Madeiras, but do not let this delude you into thinking that this great dessert wine has only a sweet taste! It has a splendid 'secondary taste' on the palate which ensures that unlike many, many types of sweet wine it can never be cloying. Many people claim that it marries very well with rich puddings, but I would advise giving it the respect it deserves by treating it solely as a dessert wine. Best of the best as a dessert, I respectfully submit, is the marriage between a glass of *Malmsey* and the sweetest of all desserts, a dish of crystallized fruits.

Of the four the first three, *Sercial, Verdelho* and *Bual* should be served slightly chilled as this brings out their finest characteristics. The fourth, *Malmsey*, should be served, like red wines, at room temperature.

Like the others *Malmsey* keeps in bottle to a very great age. In fact bottles of three hundred years and over have been sampled and proved to be still in good condition. Hence the 1789 *Tarrantez* to which I referred at the beginning of the chapter. I must also add that the *Tarrantez* is a type of grape that became almost extinct, but is again being cultivated today so we may be fortunate enough to find it on the market once more – in a few years' time.

In addition to the main four there is still to be considered an eminently drinkable Madeira wine, a fifth type called *Rainwater*. This is light in colour and usually dry enough to serve as an aperitif; it was originally blended for the American market and made from grapes grown on the highest points of the island. The name derives from the fact that there is no artificial irrigation on these heights and therefore the grapes from which it is made depend entirely upon rainfall for their moisture.

Finally, broaching slightly on my wife's preserves, fairly small libations of any of these Madeiras add great distinction to both sweet and savoury dishes, as well as to sauces and may fairly be considered as very distinguished adjuncts to fine cookery.

BRANDY AND ARMAGNAC

Brandy is an *Eau-de-Vie* (water of life) and is the distilled, fermented juice of the grape. *Eaux-de-Vie* can, in fact, be distilled from many other fruits, but the simple word 'Brandy' is generally taken to mean 'spirit' from the grape.

Brandy is made in many parts of the world but practically the only Brandy of distinguished character and real quality comes from the Cognac region of France. This is made in a very strictly defined area in the Charente around the town of Cognac and no Brandy from any other source is entitled to call itself *Cognac*.

There is no doubt whatever that the drinking of a fine old *Cognac* is one of the greatest gastronomic pleasures life can offer. It also represents the perfect ending to a good meal. Indeed too many people today commit the cardinal crime of offering a very ordinary Brandy at the end of a fine meal at which they have served fine wines.

As a great wine connoisseur once said, 'Time makes Brandy, man can only help.' But the word 'time' can be misleading. *Cognac* does not improve in the bottle. Its high alcoholic content preserves it in the same state as when it was bottled. Therefore it is matured in casks; these are made of oak from the neighbouring Limousin forests. The longer *Cognac* remains in cask, the more the colour deepens and the finer the 'bouquet' becomes, but there is a definite time limit to this process too. It is reached after forty to an absolute maximum of seventy years. The age on a *Cognac* means the cask age, so for anyone to talk of 'Napoleon Brandies' is sheer nonsense. There are in fact, firms who carry the brand name 'Napoleon', much as they might carry the name 'Lux' for soap. The names represent a brand of Brandy and a brand of soap, but they have nothing to do with the Emperor or the period in which he lived.

In addition to the existing law which defines the strict limits inside which Brandy can and may be called *Cognac*, there is a decree which governs the type of grape which may be used. This is predominately the *Folle Blanche* and the *St Emilion*. Furthermore, there is another ruling concerning the type of 'still' which may be used, and for *Cognac* to be *Cognac* the only kind permissible is called a *pot-still*.

Inside the limits prescribed by *Cognac* there are six clearly defined regions. All span out from the town of Cognac and you must understand that this is not an arbitrary matter and nobody is trying to be silly about it. The plain fact is that the soil varies in each region and this, of course, exerts powerful and varying effects upon the quality and character of the *Cognacs*. The very best is called *Grande Champagne*, which you may find a bit confusing. In fact the name has no connection with the world-famous sparkling table wine, but is the name of superb *Cognac*. It will help you perhaps to appreciate why it was chosen, as Champagne originally meant 'chalky soil'.

The second region, Petite Champagne, lies to the south of Grande Champagne surrounding the town of Jarnac. The third region is called the Borderies and lies to the west. The fourth surrounds the first three and carries the name Fins Bois. The fifth forms an outer circle and its name is Bons Bois and the vineyards on the two islands just offshore comprise the sixth region known as Bois Ordinaires or Dernier Bois.

As I have said, the finest *Cognac* is *Grande Champagne*, but alas it is fabulously expensive which is understandable as it ages extremely slowly. When it reaches its peak it is heavy, has great depth of character, and an enormously powerful aroma yet it remains fine and subtle on the palate.

Next to this in quality are the *Petites Champagnes* which age a great deal more rapidly and therefore command a lower selling price. We must understand that the majority of firms, in the interests of realism, blend *Grande Champagne* with *Petite Champagne* and sell the blendings under the name *Fine Champagne*. Once again this is a matter which is carefully controlled. In order to qualify, the

Cognac must contain an absolute minimum of sixty per cent *Grande Champagne*.

Somewhat obviously in these times, several *Cognacs* are beyond the means of the average person, so again in the interests of realism, and in order to bring *Cognac* within the reach of smaller income groups, various *Champagnes* are permissibly blended with some of either the *Borderies* (soft and full-bodied), or with the *Fins Bois* in order to provide the lusty element, for the former rather lacks finesse. Alternatively blending may be done with *Bons Bois*, which again produces the more lusty peasant element because all *Bons Bois* have a distinctly earthy character. In the order in which I have given them, each of these *Cognacs* age more and more rapidly.

Next we come to the very ordinary *Cognacs* which have in them a large proportion of *Bois Ordinaires*. There was a time when there were vintage *Cognacs*, that is to say all coming from one particular year, but this is more or less a thing of the past and today practically all are blended and comprise blendings of different years.

You are all familiar with the quote which my wife uses so often in terms of food-garnish – 'the eye must be pleased before the palate is appeased and the digestion satisfied'. It has become a 'mode' for a Brandy to be brown even as it is a fact that Brandy is a 'digestif' and this popular colour is achieved by barrelling in Limousin oaks. These give off tannin to the barrelled liquor and this is how colouring is achieved among the better *Cognacs*. In the case of the lower-priced Brandies burnt sugar is used and once you have been drinking Brandies for some time you will detect this instantly, not only in them but also in *Armagnacs* with which we shall be dealing presently. I have to tell that some firms of small conscience add vanilla to cheaper Brandies to smooth off the rougher edges of the Brandy on the palate. Deplorable!

Cognac is made from a white wine of low alcoholic content. This wine is distilled in a pot-still and distillation is based on the premiss that alcohol vaporizes at a lower temperature than water so the alcohol vapour can be condensed in another vessel leaving the water behind. The spirit from the first of the vapour is called the *Produits de Tête* (head) and is too pungent to use. By the time the temperature has risen to 68° Centigrade (170°F) the ethyl alcohol has vaporized, this is called the *Produits de Cœur* (heart) and is collected separately. It is this which eventually becomes *Cognac*. As the temperature continues to rise the stage is reached where we collect the *Produits de Queue* (tail); this is not sufficiently pungent.

At this point the pot-still – a copper pot (*Chapiteau*) – is placed over a brick furnace. From this 'still' comes a pipe which carries the vapour through to another copper vessel called the *Chauffe-Vin*. From this the pipe passes through a condenser which holds cold water, which is renewed as it heats up. As the vapour re-liquidizes it runs out from a lip into a cask. The liquid is called *Brouille* and is absolutely undrinkable, so it must be re-distilled very slowly. This process is known as the *Bonne Chauffe*. Like the first distillation, the first vapours are unfit to become *Cognac* without further purification. The *Cœur* (heart) is tapped into the Limousin oak barrels of which we have spoken already and is then ready for maturing. For quality *Cognacs* this process can take from seven to a maximum seventy years.

Gravity is a most important factor in the making of *Cognac*, so you will find that the majority of the big houses have erected their buildings on hillsides. The barrels of *Cognac* are taken to the upper floor of the blending plant and poured into big vats. Pipes conduct the liquid to other vats, passing it on the way through thick wool filters. Wooden paddles are used to blend the various *Cognacs*. When blended, the *Cognac* is run into more great vats on the lower floor and it is from here that it is finally transferred to bottles.

When selecting your *Cognac* you can do so from various generally accepted markings. As a rule, the three star mark signifies the cheapest and youngest (from three to six years old) and is perfectly good for a long drink like a Brandy and soda or for using in cooking or the mixing of punches, toddies and other mixed or heated drinks. The mark V.O. (Very Old) or V.E. (Very Extra) usually symbolizes seven to twelve years old; the mark V.S.O. (Very Special Old) denotes that the *Cognac* is between twelve and seventeen years old and V.S.O.P. (Very Special Old Pale) eighteen to twenty-five years of age, while V.V.S.O.P. (Very, Very Special Old Pale) declares that the *Cognac* is a least twenty-five years of age and may well be up to forty years old. The word 'pale' is used somewhat without justification. Depth of colour has become accepted as a mark of quality by many people, although this is not correct. The majority of these *Cognacs* are well coloured, so do not be misled by this fallacy.

HOW TO SERVE COGNAC

Cognacs should be served in medium-sized, narrow-necked glasses called *ballons* or tulips (see pp. 5 and 6). Both are glasses which are deliberately shaped – the *ballon* even more than the tulip – to preserve the nose, bouquet or aroma. Please never, never, never again as long as you live allow yourself or anyone else to warm another glass of *Cognac* (or, come to that, *Marc* or *Armagnac*) either and more especially not with those pernicious methylated spirit stoves used in pretentious third-rate restaurants. All that is ever needed to bring out the fragrance and the nuances of flavour can be obtained from the natural warmth of the human hand. Cup your hands round the glass and nurse it for a few moments until you can no longer feel the glass because it and the contents have reached blood temperature – the temperature of your hands. Then bury your nose in it and sniff up the aroma and find out that way whether I am correct or not. Mark you, there is an exception to this rule if you are an old faker and you want to palm off a bit of 'fire-water' or 'gut-rot' as a drinkable Brandy. Hold the glass over the stove and heat it very thoroughly because this will kill the basic crudities of the 'fire-water' with which you are aiming to deceive.

Finally I must tell you a little tale which appeals to me enormously, I only hope you too will enjoy it. Once upon a time there was a group of old men who met regularly at three-monthly intervals to indulge their passion for food and wine and to widen the arc of their experience. One day one old boy observed, sniffing the last bottle of a Vintage Claret, 'What a pity we do not have one young man amongst us. We are all old and shall soon be dead and with us will go all living memory of such a wine,' and he proposed that from then onwards one youngster should be invited to each dinner so that his wine memory could extend into the future far beyond those of his hosts. This was done. The young man came. His behaviour was faultless throughout the meal. He evinced curiosity and intelligent interest concerning the things he did not know, displayed a surprising amount of knowledge for his years, handled his glass correctly, nosed or smelled his wines, held them against the light to appreciate the colour and commented upon it and generally won the respect of the old boys, especially the one whose idea it had been to invite him. Came the Brandy, rare, mature, fabulous – the young man picked up his *ballon* and knocked it back! There was an appalled silence round the table. He glanced at the ring of faces. 'Gentlemen,' he said, 'I have put my foot in it. Will you please tell me what I have done that is incorrect?' His host cupped his hands round his *ballon*. 'Well,' he said, 'when you have the opportunity of enjoying a *Cognac* such as this you first warm your *ballon* with your hands, then you will hold it up to the light so as to examine and enjoy the colour, then you will warm it again in your hands and when the temperature of your hands has brought out the beautiful bouquet you will nose it.' The old man punctuated his explanation with the requisite action and at this stage lifted his nose out of the *ballon* and replaced the glass upon the table. 'And then,' he said with infinite gravity, 'you put it down and begin to talk about it.'

Just to confuse you for a moment – and then I hope all will be clear – there *is* a 'Brandy' which, when at its best, can be comparable to *Cognac*. It is called *Armagnac*, and it comes from Gascony. Gascony is, quite apart from its *Armagnac*, a fascinating province which seems to have stayed firmly rooted in the seventeenth and eighteenth centuries. Armagnac is old; it is stiff with history and among its manifold claims to fame the region contains the original home of d'Artagnan, the swashbuckling adventurer who led the Three Musketeers, Athos, Porthos and Aramis.

In fact, while the name 'Napoleon' still flourishes in *Cognac* – as a name mark you! and of no special vinous distinction – so the name 'd'Artagnan' flourishes in Gascony today and a great many of the *Armagnac*-producing houses carry the d'Artagnan mark.

What is *Armagnac*, precisely? Well, the late great M. André L. Simon said, 'A good *Armagnac* can be very good, but even the best cannot hope to approach, let alone rival, the best *Cognac*.' *Cognac* reigns supreme, but this is not to say that many a great and pleasureable experience does not lie in wait for the man or woman who takes the trouble to study *Armagnacs*.

Let me give you an example. When we left Gascony after a stay in the charming old farmhouse of the Sammalens brothers, we were given by them a magnum of 1848 *Armagnac*. Now, these brothers, quite apart from being absolutely charming, are the most fastidious and scrupulous of *Armagnac* producers and their *Armagnacs* are of the very first flight – always. Well, in due course, after it had been properly rested in our cellars, we broached this 1848 as the climax to a preceding series of very fine wines at a rather special dinner-party. It was all that we had expected it would be, but the most impressive experience attached to the drinking and enjoying of it actually came the next morning. My wife had left her handbag in the drawing room when she went to bed and she wanted something which was in it. So the very first thing the next morning, even before the curtains had been drawn, she went into the drawing room. Now there are few things which are generally more disagreeable than entering a curtained, shuttered room in which considerable drinking has been done until the small hours. Not so on this occasion, for our drawing room was still fragrant and delightful, still impregnated with the wonderful bouquet of this fine old *Armagnac*.

The nature of the soil imparts to *Armagnac* a very special character, just as it does in *Cognac*. The very best comes from the Bas-Armagnac or Lower Armagnac district, which name derives from the simple geographical fact that it is far less hilly than the rest. In fact in the centre of this area – named Le Grand Bas – the soil has a far higher proportion of sand than in any other Armagnac area and produces a much more delicate alcohol than does the rest of the district. Next to this region comes the district of Tenareze and third, in graduation of quality, the Haut-Armagnac district.

The type of grape used here is called *Picpoul*. It produces, in fact, a sour wine of rather low alcoholic content.

You must understand that the whole process of producing *Armagnac* in Gascony is far from commercial and still rooted in the past, although even here the old foot treading has given way to a kind of primitive mechanization. There are still old ceremonies and traditions which are faithfully maintained every single vintage. For example, when a new vintage hand is taken on all the girl pickers gather round him and squeeze ripe grapes all over his face and thoroughly work over him with the juice. A somewhat sticky initiation!

Once the normal pressing of the grapes is completed the juices run into underground fermenting vats and distillation begins as soon as the fermenting is completed. Now here, in this region, the distillation is carried out in portable pot-stills which are moved around from one grower to another, and very funny they look on the move, not unlike small, old-fashioned engines; they are, believe it or not, considered to have personalities of their own. Some growers still insist on having the same pot-still every year, as they

F

stubbornly maintain that all are different in character and personality and that producing a really fine *Armagnac* depends upon having
whichever is the pot-still of their choice!

There are a number of ways in which the distillation varies from
that of *Cognac*. For *Armagnac* it is a slow, continuous process and
there is only one distillation. First the wine is run into the still and
then the vapours run out into a barrel without interruption and the
flow coming from the still must be regulated to a mere trickle.
Conversely, in making *Cognac* wine is heated very gradually,
whereas in *Armagnac* it is exposed to a very hot fire at once, but in
Armagnac, as in *Cognac*, the first and last vapours are absolutely no
good at all and the finest *Armagnac* comes from the heart or *cœur*.

The colourless spirit is then put into casks which are made of
black oak from the neighbouring forests; the casks always have to
be new ones which have been seasoned for four to five years before
being used. Indeed the whole character of *Armagnac* depends upon
the peculiar properties of these black oak barrels, which are quite
different from the Limousin oak ones used in the making of *Cognac*.
Moreover, the spirit itself matures very much more rapidly than
Cognac and will be very palatable in only five years. It is generally
considered that the properties of this oak exhaust themselves in
about twenty-five years and so it is that twenty-five years has
become the maximum cask age in general rulings; but, speaking
personally and having tasted *Armagnac* of very much greater age,
I cannot agree with this fact, as it is generally accepted to be.

Even the selling becomes highly specialized and fascinating in
Gascony. The growers meet always in the same café in the same
town – the Café de France at Eauxe – and here, year after year,
they will fix their prices and meet the buyers over glasses of the
strong local wine. Each grower will produce from his pocket small
samples of his own product. The buyers rarely drink or even taste
these, they just pour a few drops into the palms of their hands, rub
their hands together and then cup them in front of their noses; all
their buying is done from the aroma thus obtained.

LIQUEURS

Let us begin by understanding precisely what we mean when we use the word 'liqueur'. In so doing we may determine together what is not meant by the word, which comes from the Latin *liquefacere*, meaning to dissolve, melt or make liquid. Thus we learn that liqueurs are sweetened spirits, flavoured by infusion or distillation with herbs, fruits, roots, nuts, seeds, leaves or flowers. They are often artificially coloured, are designed to be drunk at the end of a meal with coffee in very small quantities and are said to be very good aids to the digestion. It is probably for this reason that the French refer to liqueurs collectively as *'les digestifs'*.

Their ancestry dates back to the time of Hippocrates when in the fifth century B.C. Hippocrates distilled spirits, blended them with herbs and thus achieved beverages which were said to be extremely potent.

Five hundred years later we find records concerning a wine called *Faustino*. This was also a form of liqueur. Liqueurs, however, are not *Eaux-de-Vie* with which I have dealt in a separate chapter. It is essential that we separate them in our thinking.

The records of the Middle Ages bristle with tales about herbal wines which possessed both curative and digestive properties and it is generally accepted that liqueurs as we know them were mostly invented by the monks for these remedial purposes. Such recipes have always remained very closely guarded secrets. They may contain up to one hundred ingredients and they are so individual that even a liqueur as famous as Orange Curaçao varies from distiller to distiller by some slender change of balance, by differing proportions here, a little more sugar there, elsewhere a different variety of orange and so on. Indeed some use Brandy as a base and I shall be giving you presently a whole range of alternatives which are chosen by the various producers so as to put you fully in the picture.

In the making of liqueurs there are two main processes – distillation and infusion. Distillation, the more expensive process, is mostly employed for the very finest products. In this method the herbs, fruits and other ingredients are first 'macerated', which means softened by steeping in strong spirit. The resultant mixture is then distilled so that the alcohol and the volatile flavouring passes through the still. The fluid is then sweetened and this is when, if it is thought to be advantageous, it is also coloured.

The second method – infusion – involves adding the fruit or other flavourings to the spirit and then filtering the liquor and sweetening it. It is impossible to deny that this method, with few exceptions, produces liqueurs which are inferior to those made by distilling, but we must accept that it is unavoidable when using flavourings which are not volatile.

There is a third method, the 'essence' process, which merely means the direct addition of natural or synthetic flavouring materials to spirit, with subsequent sweetening and colouring. This method is used chiefly for the production of cheap and inferior liqueurs.

The one common factor in all liqueurs is alcohol. Alcohol is the basis of the entire range, but it varies according to the product and may well be Brandy, Whisky, Rum, natural spirit, grain spirit, fruit spirit or even rice spirit; the purity of whichever one is used being the all-important factor.

Further to this, the extracted flavouring compounds are so very strong and usually so bitter that only minute quantities of them are employed.

These too come very much under the heading 'various' or 'sundry'; they can be herbs or barks, woods, drugs, roots, flowers, seeds and fruit or even honey.

Again, the full enjoyment of a liqueur by the diner must depend upon several factors; the glass, which should be thin, clear and large enough for you to be able to appreciate the colour and bouquet; the colour of the liquid; its bouquet; the savouring upon the palate, and finally, when you have at last ingested it after all these weighty preliminaries, there is the agreeable glow set up in the stomach and the lingering after-taste to gratify the palate.

Many liqueurs are improved in flavour by chilling which reduces the sweetness but enhances the bouquet.

My wife has always insisted – although she, of course, intends only Brandy, and *Armagnac* or *Marc*, to come within her definition – that the only time when a woman should wheedle a man for something she desires excessively and which she knows will be extremely costly, is after her victim has enjoyed a really good *digestif*.

Having dealt with the making of liqueurs in general I would now like to particularize. There are so many liqueurs from all parts of the world that it would be an impossible task to enumerate them all in this book, but what I can do is divide them into six categories and deal briefly with the better known ones in each category.

HERB LIQUEURS

Benedictine is among the most famous and is an old French liqueur said to have been invented at Fécamp in 1510 by a Benedictine monk named Don Bernardo Vincelli. During the French Revolution the abbey was destroyed, but the precious recipe survived and eventually came into the hands of a M. Le Grand, who reproduced it. It is now known all over the world, often as *Dom*, the letters D.O.M. standing for *Deo Optimo Maximo* (To God, Most Good, Most Great). It is said to be beneficial for rheumatics and similar disorders. A variant of this liqueur is B and B (*Benedictine* and Brandy) which appeals to many palates as it is much drier; it was very popular with Victorians and excessively so during the Edwardian era.

Chartreuse is among the most costly besides being one of the most famous of liqueurs. Many producers have attempted to imitate it: none have ever achieved one which equals the quality of the original.

Chartreuse was first made by the Carthusian monks at their monastery at Voiron near Grenoble. In 1793 these monks were expelled, but when they went they took with them their priceless formula which consisted of around one hundred herbs, flowers and additional secret ingredients. The monks eventually returned to their monastery in 1816 where they promptly resumed *Chartreuse* production. In 1903 they were once again expelled from France and this time found refuge in Tarragona where again they immediately set about the making of more *Chartreuse*. However, the French Government had by this time confiscated their trademark and their remaining stocks; these were sold to a company who attempted imitation under the original trademark. In Spain the monks were selling the genuine article under the name *Tarragone*. In 1938 the monks once again returned to their old distillery at Voiron and again resumed production under the original name. There are two kinds of *Chartreuse*, Green and Yellow – Green is the stronger of the two at 96° proof, while Yellow rates only 75° proof. Some people consider that they should be drunk mixed, but I am not among them.

La Vieille Cure is a preparation of some fifty aromatic and root plants gathered in the Cognac and Armagnac regions. It has been produced since the Middle Ages in the Gironde and at the Abbey of Cenon.

Mille Fiori is an Italian production supposed to contain essences from one thousand flowers, hence the name. It is sold in tall, slim bottles with a small twig which has sugar crystals adhering to it inside each one. The crystals are formed by the large quantity of sugar in the mixture, some of which crystallizes on the twig as the liquid cools.

Izarra is a Basque liqueur, produced – like *Chartreuse* – in two forms, the Green at 85° proof and the Yellow at 64° proof. The base is *Armagnac* and the flavouring comes from plants of the French Pyrenees, predominantly lavender and sage.

Raspail is made at Cenon. Originated by François Raspail in 1847, it contains a large number of natural products like myrrh, angelica and calamus, which is an Eastern aromatic plant.

Drambuie means 'the drink that satisfies'. It is the oldest and best of the Scotch Whisky liqueurs. It is said to be made from a special formula of Bonnie Prince Charlie's and it is also said that after his defeat at Culloden Moor one of his followers helped him to escape to France and as a reward the Prince gave him the formula. The recipient of this bounty was a MacKinnon of Straithaid and his descendants produce *Drambuie* to this day.

Glen Mist is a much younger Scotch Whisky which is made with honey and sugar. It was invented by Hector MacDonald. At the end of the last war in 1945, when supplies of Scotch Whisky, sugar and honey were practically non-existent the production was removed

to Eire and Irish Whiskey was used as a base, but in 1963 S. F. Hallgarten resumed production in Scotland from whence comes
Glen Mist today.

Irish Mist is very similar to *Glen Mist* and as Irish Whiskey is used
in the making, the name was created to avoid confusion with the
Scottish one.

LIQUEURS CONTAINING ONE PREDOMINANT HERB

Anisette is a compound of pure spirit and sweetened aniseed.
The best known is that of the firm Marie Brizard of Bordeaux. The
company works to a secret formula which was inherited by the
original Marie Brizard. The family still own the distillery and today,
in addition to Anisette, produce a wide range of other liqueurs.

Kümmel is a favourite *digestif* to sip, especially among golf club
members. It is a caraway-and-aniseed-flavoured liqueur. As long ago as
1575 a certain Lucas Bols made it in Amsterdam; Bols is now an
enormous concern and *Bolskümmel* is still known universally, as
indeed is another, *Wolfschmidt Kümmel*.

Danzig Goldwasser is a clear liqueur of caraway and aniseed flavour
which sparkles with tiny golden flakes; these were added when it
first became known that gold had valuable medicinal properties.
During the last war the Danzig distillery was destroyed and today
all Danzig Goldwasser is manufactured in West Berlin.

Crème de Menthe (or to use the name we gave it in our youth,
'Flapper's Joy') is made by practically every producer of liqueurs.
Mint is generally accepted as one of the most valuable digestives, but
it is definitely repellent to the sophisticated palate and only popular
to very inexperienced taste-buds – hence the nickname! The one
made by Cusenier is probably the best known – it is the more usual
green colour, although there are other firms who make both green
and white.

FRUIT LIQUEURS

There are a number of fruit liqueurs. The most renowned is Cherry
Brandy, of which probably the greatest selling make is the Danish
Cherry Heering, but there are several excellent British brands on the

market. Another product of cherries is *Maraschino*, which is mostly used for cooking. It is employed in many puddings, but it also makes its appearance in mixed drinks.

Other stone fruit liqueurs are Peach Brandy, Apricot Brandy and *Crème de Prunelle* (plum). In the making of all these it is almost essential to use the stone kernels to obtain the best flavour.

There are two groups of soft-fruit liqueurs, the berries and the tropical fruits. The best berry fruit liqueurs are Blackberry (primarily Polish), Raspberry (*Crème de Framboise*), Strawberry (*Crème de Fraise*), Wood Strawberry (*Crème de Fraise de Bois*), and Blackcurrant (*Crème de Cassis*). This last is a very old liqueur which was made in the sixteenth century by the monks near Dijon.

Nor must we forget the traditional English 'Stirrup Cup' – Sloe Gin, which we have made at home with great success by steeping the picked, pricked sloes in gin and soft brown sugar and maturing for at least a year before broaching. It is a most warming drink on a cold day and can be highly intoxicating.

The tropical fruits for liqueurs include Banana (*Crème de Banane*), and Pineapple (*Crème d'Ananas*) which has a Rum base.

CITRUS FRUIT LIQUEURS

These are very well known and are chiefly variations on the Orange Curaçao theme. Only the orange peel is used in the making; this is soaked in water, then steeped in spirit and finally distilled. The best-known one is orange coloured, but is obtainable in other colours like white, blue, green and brown. There is, too, a very highly rectified White Curaçao (rectification is the process of purifying any volatile spirit by distillation) called *Triple-Sec*. *Cointreau* is the most popular trademark. Another Curaçao is *Grand Marnier*, unique because its special flavour is produced by using nothing but *Cognac* as the base spirit.

South Africa produces a citrus fruit liqueur Van der Hum made from *Naartjies* – a form of orange indigenous to this country. A number of other flavourings are added and it was most likely to have been made originally by the Dutch settlers in an attempt to reproduce *Curaçao*. The name means 'Mr What's-His-Name' – they evidently forgot the name of the inventor.

There is also *Parfait Amour*, a violet or red-coloured liqueur, very sweet, citrus-oil-based, highly scented and coriander-flavoured. If such a thing is possible this is even more sickly than *Crème de Menthe*!

BEAN AND KERNEL LIQUEURS

These are used more for flavouring than as digestives. In the case of the new *Royal Mint Chocolate*, the best definition is an after-dinner mint in liquid form. The other commonly known ones are *Crème de Cacao* made from cocoa beans, *Tia Maria* and *Kahlua*; both are coffee liqueurs. Then there is *Noyau* which tastes strongly of almonds and is made from peach and apricot kernels.

MISCELLANEOUS

In no special category is *Advocaat*, a thick, low-strength mixture of egg yolks and Grape Brandy which I consider nauseating. It is, however, immensely popular with some females who mix it with fizzy lemonade and call it a 'Snowball'. Another, which really does come under the heading of 'sundries', is *Atholl Broze*, a Scottish drink made with honey, fine uncooked oatmeal, Whisky and some other, mercifully undisclosed, ingredients. This mixture is violently agitated, bottled, corked and stored for some days. As a final *coup-de-foudre* cream is sometimes added. No comment!

EAUX-DE-VIE

Eaux-de-Vie are spirits distilled from the grape or other fruits, so, in effect, Brandy is one, but it is in a category of its own as you have already read in the preceding pages. Moreover, *Eaux-de-Vie* differ from liqueurs in that none of the former is either sweetened or coloured.

There is an *Eau-de-Vie* made from grapes called *Marc* which is distilled from the husks of the grapes after the wine has been made. It is distilled at a very high strength and when young is colourless and tastes like fire-water! However, *Marc* matures very well and an old one can be most enjoyable; like Brandy it takes on a brown colour with age. The best known are *Marc de Champagne* and *Marc de Bourgogne*, they are also generally accepted as the best. I was of this opinion until, when holidaying in the south of France one summer, we ran into that eccentric gastronomic millionaire, the late Nubar Gulbenkian and his wife, in a small but excellent restaurant. He asked us to join them for coffee and 'digestives'. He then produced a bottle which he explained was an old *Marc-de-Provence* and said that it was, in his opinion, the finest of all *Marcs*. Having tasted it, we agreed completely, so if you find yourself in that area look out for it and give yourself a treat – provided of course that you care for this type of drink. The word, by the way is pronounced MAR and not MARK. To quote from a famous Margot Asquith quip, the 'k' is silent – as she pointed out when called Margot by Jean Harlow – the 't' is silent in both!

The great *Eau-de-Vie* of Normandy is called *Calvados*, which is really much the same as the 'Apple Jack' of Devon and Cornwall. It is made in the same way as *Marc*, using apple pulp after the cider has been made. Its name derives, as you would imagine, from the town of Calvados. It is said that the Normans used to take a glass of this spirit in the middle of the meal to act as an aid to digestion and to reawaken the appetite for the ensuing service of dishes. Having studied some of the eating habits of the Normans, I can believe that they needed the stimulant. The custom is still observed; it is known as *Trou Normande*. *Calvados* should be served in small glasses and must be tossed back like Vodka or Aquavit. When drunk as a digestive after dinner, *Calvados* should, however, be sipped just like Brandy. Again, like *Marc*, when young it is not very pleasant but when mature is extremely good.

Probably the best known of all *Eaux-de-Vie* is *Kirsch* or *Kirsch-wasser*. This is produced mainly in the Black Forest area of Germany and in Alsace and Switzerland. It is distilled from the fermented juice of small, black, very juicy cherries. To make a fine one the distillation must be done very rapidly after the finish of the fermentation. It is then matured in 'demijohns' (glass or stone jars with narrow necks), not in wooden casks which would colour it. For *Kirsch* and other *Eaux-de-Vie* made from stoned fruits it is absolutely essential to introduce the kernels before fermentation and to double distill it in pot-stills. This treatment gives the finished product a slightly bitter tang.

The best known of the other stone-fruit products are *Quetsch* made from the *Swiztenplum* and the *Mirabelle* (cherry plum). In central Europe these Plum Brandies are called *Slivovitz*.

From France, Germany and Switzerland come soft fruit *Eaux-de-Vie* like *Framboise* (raspberry), *Fraise* (strawberry), *Fraise de Bois* (wood strawberries) and from Morocco and other Mediterranean countries you get one made from figs, which we found rather nasty and certainly do not wish to dwell upon!

There is also one made by France, Germany and Switzerland called *Poire William* which is distilled from William pears. This is often sold in pear-shaped bottles in which a ripe pear has been grown – the bottle actually being tied to the tree.

All these *Eaux-de-Vie* are normally drunk at the end of the meal and in France are usually referred to as *digestifs*, a very descriptive name as, in the main, to serious students of the grape in all forms, they are more of a specific to aid the digestive organs than a valued vinous experience. My opinion! Pray reject it if you so wish!

VERMOUTH

The majority of people, if asked 'What is Vermouth?' would not be able to say much beyond, possibly, 'It is something you mix with gin'. Actually Vermouth is an aperitif on its own and if mixed with spirits like gin it ceases to be an aperitif and becomes a pick-me-up. I abhor any mixed drink and will not tolerate cocktails in my own home because they ruin the palate for any food and wine that may follow and I describe them as a number of good ingredients absolutely ruined by being mixed together.

If we are to be accurate *Vermouth is wine* and the main difference between Vermouth and other wines is that Vermouth is flavoured with spices and herbs, sweetened with sugar and strengthened with pure alcohol. The name originated from the flowering shrub *Artemisia Absinthium* for which the German name is *Wermut*. France adopted this as a generic name for its aromatic wines but changed it to the French spelling 'Vermouth'.

As a matter of record, herbs, spices and plants have been added to wine since ancient Greek and Roman times and in the sixteenth century *Wermut* was added to the Rhine wines. This was never really successful and it was left to France and Italy to develop Vermouth as it is known today, which they did during the latter part of the eighteenth and the early part of the nineteenth centuries.

Vermouths of varying qualities – and not to be compared with the French and Italian – are made in other parts of the world, but the best comes from the French and Italian sides of the Alps, the French from around Lyon and Marseilles and the Italian from the Turin region. However, in my opinion the finest Vermouth of all comes from Chambéry in the Savoie. It is very dry, and lighter than most and has the distinctive flavour and smell of the summer mountain flowers which abound in this area. The French also make one that is sweeter, to which they add strawberry juice and call it *Chambéryzette*, but it is not to be compared with their main product.

METHOD OF PRODUCTION

The method of production is to take the chosen white wines, fortify the bulk up to fifteen degrees of alcohol and then expose it to the sun and rain in open casks for up to two years. The smaller proportion is fortified up to fifty degrees and *Wermut* and many other spices and herbs are macerated in the resultant liquor. The actual number and proportion is the treasured secret of each individual firm. Incidentally this mixture is also exposed in casks. Eventually the two are blended to give a mixture of seventeen per cent alcohol. Brandy is then added, which not only brings it up to the recognized alcohol strength, but also ensures its keeping quality, even after uncorking. This is an essential for folk like the Americans who are said to make dry Martinis by merely passing the Vermouth bottle over the top of the shaker!

The final process is a further period of maturing in cask for sometimes as much as five years. Then and only then is it bottled.

FRENCH VERMOUTH

French Vermouths are nearly always pale and dry and therefore dry white wines of good quality are used as a base. The white wines of the south are of the requisite quality but are slightly bitter if drunk as table wines, so that, when blended with the various herbs and spices, the particular tang emerges which is characteritistic of good French Vermouth.

ITALIAN VERMOUTH

In general, Italian Vermouths are darker in colour and sweeter than the French; in some cases burnt sugar is added to give the required colour and pure sugar to give the extra sweetness. In recent years a pale, dry Vermouth has come into being to serve the modern preference for a dry aperitif. All Italian Vermouths are compelled by law to contain a minimum of seventy per cent superior natural wine. The sweet ones must have at least fifteen and a half per cent of alcohol and thirteen per cent of sugar. The dry ones must contain not less than eighteen per cent of alcohol and a maximum of four per cent of sugar.

While Vermouth is frequently mixed with gin, it is a clean and wholesome aperitif on its own, as I have said, with the sole addition of zest of lemon peel, and I recommend it to you if you have not already tried it. It can also make a very pleasant long summer drink too when mixed with soda water, ice and a slice of lemon.

The best of the French Vermouths are made by the famous firm of *Noilly-Prat*, while the leading names in Italy are *Martini & Rossi* and *Cinzano*.

There is quite a large sale in England of British Vermouths made by two firms *Duval* and *Votrix* which although of a very different quality to the French and Italian are quite palatable and, of course, as there is no import duty they cost considerably less!

WINE MAKING IN ENGLAND

From the time of the Venerable Bede (who died in 735) grapes have been cultivated successfully in this country for a great span of years. The custom then fell into desuetude and we owe much of the renaissance of interest in viticulture today to that great *bon vivant* and diplomatist, Sir Guy Salisbury-Jones. He for many years was the doyen of our Diplomatic Corps. When Sir Guy eventually retired he devoted his great energies and experience to viticulture, and in his wake, thanks to his success, many followed until today we really do possess a small but flourishing wine industry of our own. Only recently my wife and I met a senior R.A.F. officer, on the brink of retirement, who told us that he intended investing all his capital in vineyards; fully realizing, as he admitted, that it would be at least five years before he would see any return from his money.

Meanwhile the making of home-made wines from Cowslip to Potato and from Grapefruit to Mangold continues without cessation. Many hundreds of small wine-making centres have sprung up throughout the country in the past decade, where every item needed can be obtained and where a number of excellent little books on the subject are also on sale. The present state of the poll shows that almost a million tyros have launched themselves upon the activity and are making their own wines from fruit, flowers, vegetables, leaves, dried fruits and – a habit which I do not care to endorse – from 'concentrates'. Like artificial fertilizers, my wife and I who are dedicated gardeners forswear such things with great vehemence and resolution. As an example of how remarkable is the difference in flavour between the 'artificial' and the real, we cite our present kitchen gardens. Here after six years we are virtually self-supporting, but, as always seems to happen when one has plenty of space, we have found our yields so prolific and the flavour so astonishing, by comparison with shop-bought, artificially fed and sprayed vegetables and fruit, that we recently sought out friends who would relieve us of our surplus produce. The result was staggering. Today friends come from the most distant parts of our county, and even from London, in order to obtain guaranteed compost-grown produce – sometimes in very small quantities.

Six years ago we ate some particularly succulent small grapes in Provence. My wife hoarded some pips in an air-mail envelope, then when we came home she planted them in well-soaked vermiculite in a heated greenhouse. Two years ago we had two bunches of grapes from one of the sprouted pips. Last year we had eight and at this precise moment – six years after planting – we have ninety-nine fat bunches indoors and a grape-laden outdoor vine which covers half the south wall of our, not exactly minute house. Every dead pigeon, less only its two breasts, every scrap of guts from fish and fowl has been forked into the mounds of horse manure which acts as a hot-water bottle to the roots. We have used no sprays whatever – except carefully hoarded rain-water – and, at the moment of writing, are taking it in turns to thin those bunches on which the fat little grapes are packed tightly together like passengers on a Tube train in the rush hour.

So I do recommend that, whatever wines you elect to make, you feed the plant, shrub or tree from which you take the basic material on *manure* and *natural compost* if you want full flavour. Again, we have observed, after six years of immunation from 'artificials', that the scent is returning to flowers which were totally devoid of it on a diet of 'tin' fertilizers. Admittedly the birds have returned too, but other than the pigeons and the tits, which we have to destroy in self- and crop-protection, these are an added delight, as are the butterflies which were non-existent when we came here and are now covering the buddleias.

So for Home-Made Wine First Principles I would ask you to adhere to the first and greatest trio at all times. Grow naturally; wash your feet in pure soap and then rinse well before treading, and make perfectly sure that every implement and container is spotlessly cleaned without the dubious benefit of detergents. If these three rules are followed faithfully and if you do not follow the eager-beaver road to disaster of trying to cork down your Parsnip or Elderberry wine (just for two examples) before fermentation is absolutely completed, you can be reasonably assured of a palatable beverage as a result of your labours. You should also include two other Golden Rules. Give the wine a chance to mature in bottle before broaching it, do not allow your impatience to overcome your better judgement and, if you are the merest beginner, follow a reliable recipe faithfully and without deviation at the outset.

This is the bugbear of my wife's culinary existence. We have a rule of our own concerning recipes of any kind: NOTHING PUBLISHED WHICH IS NOT FIRST TESTED. Even so, you would be astonished at the women who write in claiming that something does not work although they have done exactly as was told to them. On closer examination – for we always pursue such allegations relentlessly – it transpires that they (a) mis-read an ingredient, (b) thought it did not matter and had not any in the house and so left it out, or (c) put a small amount of something into an over-large container, thus defeating both the finished consistency and the cooking time. In one hilarious incident we were jointly challenged by just such a reader. On probing, we discovered that she lived nearby; we invited her to the house with our newspaper-published recipe; we supplied the ingredients; we supervised the making, and at the finish, when the item was seen to be perfect, the woman burst into tears, and confessed that 'I had a row with my husband and just took it out on you!'

Sixteenth-, seventeenth- and eighteenth-century cookery books abound with recipes for home-made wines and cordials and even liqueurs, of which *Capillaire* is oft-recurring. This is a liqueur made from Maidenhair Fern. Here it is a matter of knowing what a peck is, since instructions abound to 'take a peck of cowslips', and what a gallon is, and then being able to do the necessary arithmetic to subdivide to obtain less Brobdingnagian proportions – at least for the average housewife.

Again, there are a number which advise the use of 'Orange Flower Water' and 'Rose Water'. These can be pitfalls, as we found out to our cost when another angry reader made the famous chocolate pudding Crème Marie Louise after seeing us make two simultaneously on stage. It was, she claimed, 'disgusting', though she had done exactly as we had done on stage and had indeed tasted one of ours which was 'super'. The poor lady had gone to the chemist (as instructed) for both the 'waters' but had actually trotted home with, and made her pudding with, 'Orange Flower Hand Lotion' and 'Rose Water Face Cream'!

Home-made wines of the type generally referred to as 'Country Wines' fall into two main categories – those in which natural yeast exists, as it does in gooseberries, damsons and other members of the plum family, and those which are yeast-deficient, like elder flowers, parsnips and cowslips, in which case the deficiency is made up and the fermentation started with added natural (not dried) yeast.

WHAT YOU NEED FOR WINE MAKING

This is where the wine-making centres prove such a boon. You can obtain all that you need from them. You will have to have containers such as small barrels; you can at a pinch use carboys or demijohns. You will also need vessels in which to do your fermentations; I prefer earthenware for this operation. Then you will require a crusher – or your own well-washed feet – in which case you can 'tread' your elderberries, red currants, grapes, etc. As you become more ambitious, you may well wish to invest in a small wine press, as you would certainly do if you were embarking upon a small vineyard. Then come the vital trio of measures, scales and testing apparatus if you are taking the whole business at all seriously and finally the things which I group together under the heading 'Sundries'. These include taps, corkers, bottles, corks and sulphuring apparatus in the case of grapes.

None of this elementary 'chat' is intended for those who wish to embark upon wine on a commercial scale. I would regard what we have been discussing as pleasant dalliance several notches up from bathtub gin and several notches below serious wine making. Even so, it can be pleasurable, inexpensive and sometimes highly rewarding as in the case of a certain 1943 bottling of Sloe Gin, made, forgotten and rediscovered in 1958. It drank extremely well, but the Dedicated Imbiber was prone thereafter to take the stairs to bed on all fours singing happily.

You may well ask what books would I recommend to the serious student? My answer is . . . start modestly by investing in two: *Wine Growing in England* by George Ordish, published by Rupert Hart-Davis, and *First Steps in Wine Making* by C. J. Berry, an 'Amateur Winemaker' Publication, of which the author is the editor. I dare not quote the prices on either because no prices ever seem to remain constant for more than a few weeks in these troubled and difficult times.

When tackling specific recipes for home-made wines I feel we must give pride of place to a very simple family receipt of so great an age that its origins are lost to us today. It produces what our great grandparents called Elderflower Champagne. This recipe is not only easy but also speedy; it may be made, bottled and drunk after three days. The one arbitrary bit about it is that it has a very short making season – when the Elder trees are in flower. It is not essential to drink it when freshly made; this we can state with absolute confidence, since the head of our kitchens, Sally Ascher, whom many of you will have seen with us on stage and on television, tucked half a dozen bottles away so carefully that she actually forgot all about them and only this year, just before the elderflower blossom time came round again, we accidentally discovered them in a cold, dark corner of a little-used cupboard. Convinced that the stuff would now be undrinkable, we broached it, only to find it tasted exactly as when it was freshly made. So you may regard this beverage as having at least a year's life in bottle – if you can manage to keep it that long. It is immensely popular with both young and old in very hot weather.

ELDERFLOWER CHAMPAGNE

Ingredients

4 large elderberry flower heads, 1½ lb preserving sugar, 2 teasp. white wine vinegar, 1 gallon cold water, 2 lemons.

Method

Squeeze halved lemons – quarter each half of peel. Put into earthenware container with all remaining ingredients. Stir thoroughly. Cover thickly. Give occasional further stirrings for twenty-eight hours. Strain, bottle and drink after seven days.

COOKED WINE

This is a vinous curiosity found in Monsieur M. Hav's *Dictionnaire des Ménages* in 1820.

Use white grapes. Cover the available quantity with cold rain-water. Bring to the boil slowly and skim with extreme care. Continue simmering and skimming until only one-third of original fluid remains. Tip into cold, open-necked containers (vases) to chill. Agitate with a vine stick continuously to evaporate the steam. (Failing a vine stick, then a copper spoon may be used.) Once the 'wine' is cold, tip it into a small barrel and 'bung' securely. Leave until the month of November. Then clarify with egg whites. Put four unbeaten eggs to a 4½ gallon barrel and beat with a vine stick dropped down the bung-hole. Re-bung and leave until all sediment has sunk to base and wine is crystal clear. At a moment of sharp frost, strain into bottles, cork down and 'bin'.

TO MAKE REAL VINEGAR

The word vinegar comes from the French – *Vin-Aigre* – which means soured wine. This will explain to any youngster why that malt stuff is banned by bell book and candle from the kitchens of any experienced cook. *It is not vinegar*, for it is made with malt!

Throughout the spring and summer accumulate in a very small barrel all the lees left in wine bottles and any wines which have inadvertently been left uncorked after broaching. Stuff a handful of young, green vine leaves in, affix bung and set in a sunny corner which has a south aspect. Throughout the summer add and remember to shake and turn regularly twice a week. In September strain through four folds of muslin and the result will be *pure vinegar*.

Note: The addition of peeled garlic cloves, handfuls of fresh tarragon leaves or any other chosen herbs *after* the vinegar is completed and to single bottles will ensure the cook a regular supply of tarragon, garlic and other herb vinegars.

CHERRY BRANDY

Ingredients

6 lb black cherries, 7 lb Morello cherries, ½ gallon (4 pints) common Brandy, soft brown 'pieces' sugar, loaf sugar.

Method

Mash or squeeze the cherries in the hands and, after stalking, place in an earthenware container and cover with given Brandy. Cover container with aluminium foil and then a thick fold of blanket. Leave forty hours, then press in a canvas bag until every drop of juice has been extracted. Taste, sweeten with brown sugar and some restraint, remembering that sweetening will develop in the ensuing months, replace foil, insulating covering, and then blankets. Leave in a cold place, preferably on stone slab for four weeks, strain, bottle and add a lump of loaf sugar to each (litre) bottle before corking down. Store bottles upright.

Here is an example from the days when recipes were receipts and quantities were given to suit households of perhaps sixty or seventy persons.

TO MAKE SMYRNA RAISIN WINE

'To an hundred pounds of raisins put four and twenty gallons of sweet water. Let it stand covered for fourteen days and then put it into your cask [note the singular 'cask'!]. After it has continued there six months put a gallon of Brandy to it and bottle it as soon as it is fine.'

Note: Wine making was so familiar a part of the domestic duties that it was unnecessary to deal in more detail with the racking and straining, the bottling and corking than is given in the phrase 'bottle it as soon as it is fine'.

Red Currant Wine we have drunk and it is very refreshing on a hot day if served very well chilled. Here is a slightly more practical recipe but still of antique origin.

RED CURRANT WINE

Pick only absolutely ripe red currants on a really dry day. Strip
the berries from their stalks into a roomy wooden bowl and then
bruise them with a wooden pestle. The pusher supplied with modern
electric mincers does very well for this purpose. Leave them to
ferment and from the onset of fermentation allow twenty-four
hours. Turn them on to a hair sieve and leave them without any
pressure to drip back into your wooden bowl. Measure the liquor.
Allow 2½ lb of modern preserving sugar to every eight pints. Stir,
and finally stir in two pints of common Brandy. This may well be
done in a carboy in which case the neck top should be stopped with
lamb's wool. Stand, preferably on a stone slab, for six weeks. Test
with a pipette for clarity and when the wine is absolutely clear
strain and bottle it. Affix corks lightly but do not stopper down for
a further fourteen days.

COWSLIP MEAD

Cowslips were one of the foremost subjects for the making of both
wine and mead. Clearly they were more abundant in our ancestors'
times, but they are still to be found – especially in the south-western
counties of England. When you find them take as many as will pack
down four times into a quart measure with 1 lb 6 oz of honey, half
a gallon of rain-water, half a large lemon, one very small sprig of
sweetbriar and a rounded teasp. of brewer's yeast. Dissolve sugar
in water, reduce by simmering to three pints, skim well. Pour two
pints only upon the cowslips and let them stand overnight. Then
slice the half lemon into the remaining honeywater, stir in and add
both yeast and sweetbriar. Stir well. Cover with a thick piece of
blanket and leave six days. Strain into a small barrel. Leave six
months then strain and bottle.

DAMSON WINE

We used to be given thimblefuls of this by our old Nanny who
fancied herself as a wine maker extraordinary. She was also extremely

fussy about which damsons she used and could be heard pontificating about 'real damsons' by which, according to modern standards the old dear meant damson plums. Weigh and bruise your chosen fruit. Put 8 lb in a stone barrel with a tap. Allow a gallon of water to every 8lb. Pour, boiling over the bruised damsons. Stand two days. Draw off the liquor into a small barrel. To every gallon add 5 lb of wine crystal sugar (the stuff which is on strings). Affix barrel's bung very tightly. Keep in a cool place (ideally a cellar) for a calendar year. Strain and bottle, placing a piece of loaf sugar in each bottle. It may be drunk after two months in bottle – according to Nanny who was, after all, Hoyle to us!

TURNIP WINE

My wife tells me that this was the beverage she was offered every time she accompanied her mother on visits to the cottagers on their land. Out of the corner cupboards would come the precious bottles and more often than not the minute, thimble-sized glass mugs would be unhitched from a tiny wooden 'drinks' barrel. As Fanny recalls today it was very 'swimmy' to drink, by which I gather she intends to imply that the tiny overheated 'front rooms' had a marked tendency to revolve.

For this drink a small press is needed. The old receipt runs, take a hundredweight of small firm, preferably round turnips, peel them carefully, then slice them up small and put them in the press. When all the juices have been forced out measure and add 3 lb of loaf sugar to every gallon of juice in a wooden container only just large enough to hold the quantity. Cover with a piece of blanket for seven days by which time it should be 'working' well. When fermentation ceases turn into a barrel, bung it down tightly for three months. Test with a pipette for clarity. When absolutely clear bottle and cork down. Keep a further six months before drinking.

THE FLOWING BOWL

Our ancestors recoursed to internal central heating in the days when the only external form consisted of warming pans filled with hot embers. With these alone they offset the icy chill of their bedchambers and the stored dampness of their bed coverings. Let us not forget that any ordinary, modern blanket, used in an un-heated room can retain many pounds of water. So they drank hot wines and cordials from napkin-wrapped goblets and many are the colourful 'receipts' which have survived intact from those, er, 'good old days'.

We know of few which are not copyable – at considerably higher expenditure than when they were first created, but, curiously enough, one of these is an old family 'receipt' of my wife's to whom it came down the generations from its originator Catherine Parr who brewed it for King Henry VIII in his dotage. Originally it was made with a herb infusion, an early form of the French *tisanes*. This was mixed with Brandy, Rum, various herbs, spices and honey. Later, after the introduction of tea to England the green tea of China replaced the *tisane* and still later the honey was replaced by sugar. It is now so costly that we can only afford to serve it on very special occasions. Everyone who has drunk it has clamoured for the recipe, which is about the only one in our vast collection which we will not give – it is a family secret. I merely mention it to stress the fact that given the means all our ancestors' brews are available to us still. I need only add that I have restricted my selection to the less costly ones!

The most commonly used in bygone days had as its components a steaming kettle of boiling water, fresh lemons, and the soft brown sugar which must not be confused with 'demerara' and is called 'pieces' in the trade. We submit that Whitworths supply the best today. To these you must add Rum and butter. Some years ago we discovered just such a set-up on the bar of the famous old Beetle and Wedge Hotel at Moulsford. The then landlord (long departed) told us that in winter he did a roaring trade in 'Buttered Rum', notably with people suffering from colds. To make this felicitous brew put a two-finger depth of Rum in a tall glass. Add a small walnut of butter, a heaped teaspoonful of soft brown sugar and the strained juice of a lemon, then top up with boiling water, drop in a leaf of lemon peel and cut very thinly, stir well and drink slowly.

The simplest brew of all is basic, nose-tingling, tum-warming 'Mulled Wine'. For this you require 1 bottle of red 'plonk' wine, fourteen to sixteen lumps of sugar, an orange stuck with six cloves, half a thinly sliced unpeeled lemon, a flat eggspoon each of powdered cinnamon and of powdered ginger, one dried, torn bay leaf and the strained juice of half a lemon. Place all ingredients in a pan and raise to just below boiling-point; on no account allow the mixture to boil!

Serve in napkin-wrapped glasses (goblets or tumblers) and pray remember to insert a silver spoon in each before pouring, lest you crack the glasses and thereby lose the contents as well as the container.

The next stage up the hot wine scale is to take the above basic recipe and by additions transform it into 'Flaming Mulled Wine'. Assemble all the ingredients given for Mulled Wine. In addition have ready $\frac{1}{4}$ pint Brandy and $\frac{1}{4}$ pint mixed fresh orange and lemon juice. Heat the wine as given in the preceding recipe, omitting the sugar but adding in the orange and lemon juice. When the wine is hot place the given sugar in a punch bowl or similar container. Pour on the warmed Brandy, set light to it and quickly bruise the sugar into the flaming Brandy to crumble it. Then, while you stir to keep the flames going, ask someone to pour in the wine. Do this if possible in the darkness and, as the wine is added, lift ladlefuls in the air and let them fall back in a thin stream, then stir and repeat during all of which operation the flames will continue burning and sparkling in the darkness. When you have had sufficient of this ploy, stop ladling and stirring. Then the flames will die out and you may ladle the mixture into napkin-wrapped glasses.

COLD MILK PUNCH

Ingredients

3 lemons, 1 flat eggsp. powdered cinnamon, the same of ground nutmeg, 5 oz castor sugar, 5 fl oz boiling milk, 2½ fl oz Brandy, 15 fl oz Rum, 5 fl oz boiling water.

Method

Peel lemons thinly and strain all the juice. Steep the peel in the given Rum (under a thick fold of blanket) for twenty-four hours. Then remove covers and add Brandy, cinnamon, nutmeg and sugar. Stir until every grain of sugar is dissolved. Add the boiling milk which will curdle the mixture. Stir in the boiling water, re-cover and leave once more for twenty-four hours. Then strain through an ordinary sieve into which has been laid four folds of butter muslin. Bottle and cork down securely. Leave a minimum of fourteen days before broaching.

GRAND OLD ENGLISH WASSAIL BOWL

Ingredients

¼ pint cold water, 1 level teasp. powdered nutmeg, 1 level teasp. powdered ginger, 3 cloves, ¼ teasp. powdered mace, ½ teasp. allspice, one 2-inch stick of cinnamon, 1 lb preserving or granulated sugar, ½ bottle Brown Sherry, ½ bottle Malmsey or Bual Madeira (or use 1 whole bottle of Sherry or Madeira), 1¾ pints of old ale, 6 very small eating apples, 6 standard eggs.

Method

Core and bake apples at Gas Mark 2 or Electric 325°F for 20 mins in a dry tin. Place water, spices, sugar, chosen fortified wine or wines and ale in a thick pan and allow to become piping hot over a moderate heat, but do not allow to boil. Meanwhile, separate the eggs. Whip the whites very stiffly and whip up egg yolks lightly with a fork – just to break them down. Fold yolks gently into stiff whites with a rubber or plastic spatula, then scoop the finished foam into a punch bowl. Pour the heated brew on very slowly with one hand while whisking briskly with the other, a professional-loop whisk is far and away the easiest to use for this. At the moment of service slide apples into the brew and carry to table.

NEGUS

This sweetened, spiced, wine-mixture was originally made with Port but other unfortified red wines may be used when wishing to be somewhat more economical.
Examples: Tuscan (Italian) red wine, French red Bordeaux (Claret to us), Spanish Claret-type or Bordeaux-type.

Ingredients

1 bottle Port or other red wine, sugar and grated nutmeg to taste, grated rind of 1 lemon, the strained juice of 2 lemons, 1 pint boiling water.

Method

Heat wine without allowing it to boil. Place sugar, lemon and spices in a heated, heat-resistant jug. Add hot wine and stand brew in this container near a fire. Add boiling water, stir very thoroughly and after thirty minutes (remembering to turn the jug) pour into napkin-wrapped glasses.

ROYAL PUNCH

Ingredients

¼ pint loaf sugar, 2 pints cold water, bottle Rhine wine, ¼ bottle Beaujolais, 4½ fl oz white Rum, the grated rind of both 1 lemon and 1 orange. The strained juice of same.

Method

Place water in a thick pan over a moderate heat. Dissolve sugar completely, stirring occasionally and do not allow mixture to boil. Add grated citrus rinds. When mixture looks nice and clear raise

to a slow rolling boil and then reduce, by simmering down, to
one pint of liquid. Add in wines and Rum, raise to just below boiling-
point, add citrus juices and ladle into napkin-wrapped glasses.

SWEDISH GLOGG pronounced (roughly!) – Glurg

The traditional recipe used Sherry, but Burgundy- or Claret-type
table wines may be substituted today. This is an accommodating
brew which, if any remains after a bout of hospitality, may be bottled, corked down securely and kept until next required. The mixture
is then reheated to just below boiling-point before serving. Just as
well too, we add, since the recipe is not exactly economical!

Ingredients

1 pint low-priced, very ordinary Brandy, 1 pint Italian red wine,
French Bordeaux (Claret) or Spanish Claret-type, 5 oz loaf, preserving or granulated sugar, 6 cloves, one 2-inch stick cinnamon, $2\frac{1}{2}$ oz
blanched, unsalted almonds, $2\frac{1}{2}$ oz seeded raisins.

Method

Place all ingredients save wine in a thick pan and warm a little
over a good heat. Tip into heat-resistant bowl or punch bowl, set
mixture alight with Swan Vestas match or taper and stir until sugar
is completely dissolved. Stop stirring. Flames will subside. Add
heated (but not boiled!) wine, stir well and serve.

CHURCHWARDEN

Ingredients

1 lemon, 6 cloves, 1 bottle Tuscan red wine, Red Bordeaux or
Spanish Claret-type, 1 pint weak, scalding hot tea which *should*
be China tea, sugar to taste.

Method

Prod cloves into lemon. Place on heat-resistant plate in oven, at
Gas Mark $\frac{1}{4}$ or Electric 250°F and leave until lemon begins to turn

light brown. Heat wine without boiling. Immerse roasted lemon in wine, add hot, strained tea and sugar to taste. When sugar has dissolved completely raise heat to just below boiling-point and serve instantly.

WINE POSSET

This, I discovered in an ancient family 'receipt' book, was referred to by the author as 'a very reviving dose'!

Ingredients
1 pint sweet, new milk, ¼ pint dry white wine, 1 generous pinch each of powdered cinnamon, bay and lavender leaves (dried), the grated rind of ½ lemon, castor sugar to taste.

Method
Place milk, peel and wine together in a thick pan. Heat until the milk curdles – as it will! Strain off the whey through a butter-muslin lined sieve then dissolve sugar in whey. Stir in spices and herbs, rub curd through ordinary sieve, beat vigorously into whey mixture. Serve at once.

A GOOD MULLED WINE SPICE MIXTURE TO STORE

Ingredients
1 oz powdered cinnamon, 1 oz ground nutmeg, 1 oz powdered cloves, ½ oz ground ginger, 1 inch of a very dry vanilla pod ground to powder.

Method
Sift all together and store in an airtight container.

LEMON BRANDY

For 1 Serving: Slice the top from a medium firm, thin-skinned lemon. Scoop out every scrap of pith and flesh with a grapefruit knife. Fill up with slightly warmed Brandy, Marc or Armagnac. Set it alight, place in the top of a very small wineglass and, balancing a lump of sugar on a fork, hold this just over the surface and allow the flames and a whisper of the Brandy beneath to dissolve the sugar. When it collapses stir well, pierce the lemon amidships with a skewer thus causing the liquor to drip down into the supporting glass. When the lemon is dry, discard and sip the wineglass's contents slowly.

SNAPDRAGON

This is the Name of the Game, or at least it was in olden times when it was also known sometimes as 'Flapdragon'. The 'game' consists of snatching seeded raisins from a bowl of flaming spirit and all must be done in a darkened room. Classically the spirit should be Brandy. However, when having to sustain flames around a plum pudding at the Royal Albert Hall some years ago for nine minutes we recoursed to some unorthodox experimenting. We discovered that Vodka should be used as well in the proportions 1 part Vodka to 2 parts Brandy in order to maintain burning for a long time. Vodka has an extremely high alcoholic content, moreover it is both odourless and tasteless when heated anyway and therefore does not impair the taste of Brandy. Of course, the flavour of each snatched raisin is considerably enhanced if you find yourselves a large, screw-topped jar, well in advance of playing the game and steep the raisins in the Brandy-Vodka mixture for at least two hours before warming and igniting.

ORDINARY WASSAIL BOWL

Ingredients

3 pints brown ale, ½ lb preserving or sifted icing sugar, ½ a nutmeg, grated down, ¾ a rounded teasp. powdered ginger, ¾ pint Brown Sherry, two 1 inch thick slices of toast, 1 small, very thinly sliced (unpeeled) lemon.

Method

Warm the beer. Stir in chosen sugar, stir until dissolved, then add ginger, Sherry and lemon slices. As mixture approaches boiling-point float toast on top of brew and plunge in a red-hot poker. Turn off heat. Hold poker absolutely vertically and allow its immense heat to churn and seethe the mixture until it begins to subside. Ladle into warmed, napkin-wrapped goblets, sprinkle with a little extra nutmeg.

HEALTH AND LONGEVITY

We should all be fools if we failed to accept that a percentage of the human race regards drinking as sinful and deleterious and quotes Holy Writ in this respect. This is at best a very silly game because wine lovers can riposte with opposing quotes from the Good Book such as 'Wine which maketh glad the heart of man', and so on *ad infinitum*. We are all fully aware of the perils concomitant with excessive wine drinking and equally aware that *good* wine, whether modest or magnificent, if taken in moderation, is very good indeed for those of us who are fortunate enough to enjoy normal good health.

The French have a typical saying, 'Claret is for longevity and Burgundy for *l'amour*' – which you do not need me to translate! Fanny and I know more lusty old boys in their nineties who subsist almost entirely on bread, cheese, garlic, fruit and Clarets (red Bordeaux) than we can possibly count. Therefore, we borrow and then distort, the quote about the apple-a-day and say instead that 'a glass of good red wine every day undoubtedly keeps the doctor away and prolongs life'.

When it comes to the very young, a glass of wine, as any doctor will confirm, will do them far more good than a glass of any hard liquor. Moreover, hard liquor is an artificial stimulant, whereas wine relaxes. This is why I have always maintained that wine, when taken in moderation, irons out the creases in our daily lives. Conversely when we, in any age group, drink hard liquor at the end of the day at any kind of 'drinks' party we find that, although we may well have been hungry when we started, our appetite has diminished in ratio to the amount of hard liquor or mixed drinks containing hard liquor which we absorbed. By the time we do sit down to eat, we have killed both our taste-buds and our appetite. Hard liquor is lethal to the palate and damages the taste-buds.

I have always felt that the reason why America has such dreadful, tasteless food – eighty per cent of which is *ersatz* – is because they are not capable of recognizing the finer nuances of taste due to their excessive national consumption of hard liquor before meals.

Let us suppose that you have a member of your family who has a tendency to anaemia and needs iron in their diet. We have such a young man in our team and we try to give him, like ourselves, a glass of red wine every evening because its natural virtues are increased by a high incidence of iron. This is what is needed for this particular condition as is liver – when properly cooked! All too often it is over-cooked and thus becomes useless! Until very recently we enjoyed the friendship of a very young man of one hundred called Sir Harry Brittain. He was without doubt one of the most active men of his age we have ever known. He re-married, very delightfully, a few years ago and the only time we ever saw him was when we caught up with him just coming back from or just leaving again on another world trip – lecturing, broadcasting, wining, dining but never smoking! Of course, he had drunk good wine in moderation all his life. Fanny and I gave a dinner-party for him on his eightieth birthday. At 8.30 p.m. when he arrived in the first-floor drawing room of our London house, dear Harry was breathless, tetchy and a little deaf. He had been working all day and was clearly tired. By midnight, when dinner reached its conclusion, he had drunk several glasses of the wines which I had chosen to accompany and complement the several courses Fanny had cooked; Harry was by this time right back on form and talking brilliantly. Fanny decided to keep everyone in the dining room for coffee and Brandy. She had all the lights turned out and in the candlelight the conversation turned to law and advocacy. Sir Harry pushed back his chair, re-settled himself, looked across at the youngster facing him and began, 'Of course, you are all far too young to remember Lord Birkenhead when he was F. E. Smith but I . . .' He then launched himself on a brilliant dissertation, unfolding with his words those splendid years when he was young. His memory was unimpaired, his phrasing brilliant and he spoke for

G

twenty minutes. Alas, he only just made his 'century' and has now moved on. We and all his friends miss him tremendously.

Finally, of course, there was our Master, or, as we prefer to call him, our gastronomic Papa – the late M. André L. Simon, the Grand Old Man of wine and gastronomy. He was ninety-three when we gave his last big luncheon in honour of this event. He travelled forty-five miles in a heat-wave, revived himself on arrival with a couple of preliminary glasses of Champagne, ate lustily of six different courses, had two glasses of each complementary wine and wound up with a *ballon* of Old Brandy. Then he began talking . . . about wines and their histories. That luncheon ended on our terrace at 5.45 p.m.

Throughout the areas where red Bordeaux (Claret) and red Burgundy are produced this story is so familiar that it is 'old hat', not only concerning the great authorities of wine and wine production but also of the simplest of the men who work in the vineyards and in the cellars. Wine has no social divisions, it is classless and the same longevity prevails among the hard-handed old boys who work in the fields as amongst the white-haired ones who wear the tiny red ribbon of the *Légion d'honneur* in their buttonholes. This is, above all, why I want you to know as much as possible about wines which can be drunk today so that, for comparatively modest expenditure, you can live long and enjoy life more through drinking honest wines.

A WISE MAN TALKS
ABOUT WINE

Mr Ronald Avery, who is the head of a very great wine house, is known affectionately to his intimates as the 'Last Great Eccentric' of the wine world. He is over seventy now. He has the vitality of an electric eel, the memory of an elephant, one of what are probably the best four palates in the world today and is, besides an extrovert and a master of the *non sequitur*. In consequence, any conversation with him is apt to find his auditor both mentally and physically squinting in the attempt to hold on to the main thread – to which he always returns – after the most wild forays into the irrelevant!

He was educated at a public school, then went to Oxford. Immediately he came down from Varsity – already dedicated to drinking fine wines at all opportunities – he studied the subject under the aegis of another very great wine house who specialized in only the finest wines, and here he said, 'I learned a tremendous lot, particularly about Burgundies.'

At which point, and as perhaps his most classic *non sequitur*, he suddenly announced that he spent his holidays cycling around the vineyards of France.

'I would do about ten miles in the morning on my bicycle,' he explained. 'I was a very *young* man then! Then I would taste wines and lunch in some wine *château*. Then I would have a little sleep under a tree or hedge and cycle on into the early evening.'

Having contributed this information, he went on to talk of the rest of his life which has been very liberally spent between his family's firm and the vineyards of the world.

I asked him about specializing. I said, 'You do agree, Ronald, do you not, that no man can be an authority on all wines?' and won an explosion of indignation from him.

He replied, '*One must specialize to know.* I have become known chiefly for Clarets and this is the particular wine on which I am regarded as something of an authority, but, technically, what has always fascinated me is Burgundy. Genuine fine Burgundies are becoming rarer and rarer and there are some preposterous fakes around.'

He then fixed me with an intense stare and said, 'That reminds me, I must buy a bicycle,' which I worked out as meaning that he wanted to tour the vineyards again, if, perhaps, a little more slowly than in the manner of his youth.

He promptly reverted to talking about his work with his firm. It seems that after a few months his old Head Clerk, a great personality and a splendid man in his own right, said to him, 'I shouldn't hang about here if I were you. You will be far better off and will learn far more if you get out on the road and sell.'

On this advice and armed with the Head Clerk's list of Mr Avery's famous uncle's contacts in the wine world (and possibly with that bicycle, though history does not relate) he set out to sell his own wines and has been doing so ever since.

His earliest shopping lists read like the pipe-dreams of the wine buyers of today. He bought Burgundies. There was very little demand for Clarets in the twenties. Imagine selling to the public today cases of *Château Latour* '23 and '29 at £3.60 per dozen, or 30p per bottle. You cannot even buy 'plonk' today for that price. He then ordered me, wagging an authoritative finger at me over dinner at the Garrick Club, 'Tell your readers that in those days I only had to stick 5d on that 6s for duty! Whereas, as you know, you can buy plenty of good 'plonk' at 10p or 15p per bottle in France, but when it comes over here the unfortunate wine merchant has to stick on 30p for duty.'

Again he grasshoppered, but I managed to sort it all out and will give it to you in some sort of sequence. He spoke of buying against current advice when he was young and reaping a rich harvest for so doing. Nearly everyone advised him to buy heavy wines on the grounds that they were better stayers. He said 'pooh!' to this and developed his own theory that the lighter wines of charm and distinction more often than not outlast the heavy wines. Here he instanced the 1923s which matured very fast, so much so that you could drink and enjoy them after only three years in bottle. So the general advice was to drink them quickly; he merely stored them and waited. They lasted splendidly and, of course, appreciated in value and were sold many years later, at considerable profit, as he reminded me. The same thing happened with the '52s and '53s; the '52s being the lusty ones and the '53s the lighter wines. Enough years have passed by now to prove that the lighter '53s outstayed the lustier '52s and again these light chaps appreciated enormously in value.

I asked this Confucius of the wine world to give me some information which was relevant to the people who are buying today. He said, 'The same thing is going to happen with the wines of 1970. The wines are growing in stature in cask. They are less expensive than the '69s and they will surprise many people with their lasting power and their quality.'

He also said some very rude things about beer which he referred to as 'brewer's trash' and he rejoiced that 'The young are drinking far more wines than ever before instead of that brewer's trash. Highly recommendable! and cheaper too, in spite of the heavy tax.'

'A lot of the lower-priced wines – sold in quantity – are certainly drinkable, but do remember that by paying 5p more per bottle you can buy good wines instead of just "plonk" ', he said.

'I hold the poseur in the utmost contempt. He is the man who lays down the law about what you can drink with this and what you can drink with that. There is such a vast interest with the young that this stupid type puts them right off. When they ask me I tell them, "Drink what you like, my boy!" It is not wholly true to say that everyone's palate changes as they become experienced wine drinkers. There are men and women who will never lose their so-called "flapper's taste" for sweet wines and will drink them all their lives. Why the devil can't the so-called experts be sympathetic and recommend to them what they will like?'

I then asked him to advise those of you who are just about to embark on your first adventures in restrained wine drinking and he urged you to, 'Begin by buying half-bottles of say twenty-four different wines, twelve white and twelve red. Make notes as you drink them; go back over your notes when you have completed this comparative tasting and pick out the ones you liked best. For pity's sake never be diffident about your taste, even if you think it conflicts with those non-expert experts. Stick to your guns. As your opportunity of drinking widens your vinous outlook, you will find it fascinating to compare your initial notes. Keep 'em – and just see how your taste has developed.'

Finally let me share one little gem with you. When I rang Mr Avery up to arrange this meeting he said, 'Oh hello, Johnnie. I suppose you have rung up to ask for another subscription for the Conservative Party (for the record I have never asked him for any). Well I am keeping the money, so don't waste your time. I am going to use it to teach Harold Wilson how to eat and drink.' In the next sentence he asked, 'When are you coming sailing on my boat, and with all your money (!) why the devil didn't you come down to Bristol by helicopter to see me . . . and you had better come to dinner with me at the Garrick.'

When we had ended this dinner he tossed down his napkin and said musingly, 'I wonder if I am too old now to ride a bicycle.'

WINE TERMS YOU SHOULD KNOW

Aged: Matured wine, well developed.

Appellation Contrôlée: Controlled name (or title). Guarantees the wine to be from a specific region.

Auslese: Specially selected grapes (German).

Bas: Lower, as applied to region.

Beeren-Auslese: Individually selected choice grapes.

Beverage Wine: Normal table wine.

Bianco: White (Italian).

Bin: The place or structure in which bottles of wine are stored in a cellar.

Blanc: White (French).

Blanco: White (Spanish).

Blend: Mixing of several types, qualities or vintages to obtain a consistent standard or a particular flavour.

Bodega: A Spanish wine warehouse or store.

Body: Density.

Bond: Wines and spirits kept by the Customs and Excise until the duty has been paid are said to be 'in bond'.

Bottle Sickness: A passing ailment which affects some still wines after bottling. Time will usually cure this.

Bottle Stink: A rather unpleasant odour usually caused by wine that has grown too old.

Bouchon: Cork.

Bouchonné: French term for a wine spoiled by a faulty cork.

Bouquet: The scent of a wine.

Bourgeois: The name used for a great number of Médoc wines not classified among the great growths.

Bouteille: Bottle.

Breathe: A wine is said to breathe when it comes into contact with the air after the cork is drawn.

Brut: Very dry (Champagne), but still a little less dry than the 'Extra Dry' on the English market.

Cave: A cellar.

Chai: A storage place above ground for the wine in cask, as distinct from the cellar for the bottled wine.

Chambré: Word used to describe the condition of red wines brought to room temperature.

Château-bottled: Wine bottled at the castle or estate where grown.

Commune: French parish (smallest French administrative area.)

Corky: The mouldy smell or taste of a wine affected by a faulty cork.

Côte: Hillside, applied to wine regions.

Cradle: The wicker or wrought-iron basket often used for the serving of red wines or Port.

Cru: Growth or quality.

Crust: Deposit thrown by red wines in the bottle.

Cuve: Vat.

Cuvée: Contents of a vat.

Demi-sec: Semi-dry wine.

Dessert wine: A sweet full-bodied wine for the dessert course, such as Brown Sherry, Madeira, or Sauternes.

Domaine-bottled: Similar to *château*-bottled but used mainly in Burgundy.

Dry: As opposed to sweet flavoured wine.

Eau-de-Vie: Alcohol. Name used for Brandy or other spirit such as *Marc*, etc.

Fermentation: A process by which grape juice is converted into wine.

Filtering: A process of passing wine through a filter to render it clear. Frequently used in this country for white wines.

Fine Champagne: A Brandy from the centre of the Cognac country.

Fortification: The process of adding Brandy or some such spirit to Port and kindred type wines to increase the alcoholic content.

Frappé: Time off here for a story. The scene was the Temple des Gourmets Restaurant, Zürich. I had reached the Brandy stage. It was a very hot night. Michel, a gargantuan chef in a high bonnet, sat down in the restaurant to his own supper. Into the quiet room walked two diffident Englishmen and one equally diffident Englishwoman. The waitress spoke only French and German, the English only English. Much gesticulation ensued. I overheard three words: Brandy, *frappé*, and Crème de Menthe. A pause ensued. A frightened waitress whispered into the ear of Michel. He rose in formidable fury and cried aloud, '*Nom de Dieu*, not even for the English will I *frappé* my beautiful Brandy!' That is what happens when you do not know what to order; the men wanted Brandies and the woman a Crème de Menthe *frappé*. *Frappé* means iced or chilled. Now back to work.

Goldbeerenauslese: Selected from the ripest fruit.

Goût: Taste.

Grand Cru: Great growth.

Haut: High, usually applied to a region, but not necessarily so (Haut Sauternes has no regional significance).

Impériale: A large green French bottle holding from eight to nine ordinary bottles of Claret.

Jeroboam: Bottle equal to four of standard size.

Kabinett wein: Specially selected wine (German).

Lees: Deposit in a wine cask.

Lodge: Portuguese wine warehouse or store.

Magnum: Double-sized bottle.

Marc: Strong spirit distilled generally from grape husks.

Mousseux: Sparkling.

'*Must*': Juices of the newly gathered grapes.

Nature: Name used to describe a wine that has not been sweetened.

Petillant: Slightly sparkling wines.

Phylloxera: American wine louse which spread to practically every vineyard in the world and created enormous havoc towards the end of the nineteenth century. It has been conquered to a very great extent by grafting the vine on to American briars which are practically immune.

Quinta: The Portuguese equivalent to the French *châteaux* or *domaines*.

Racked: The process by which wine, being drawn off into new casks, is separated from its own lees.

Rehoboam: Bottle containing the equivalent of six standard bottles.

Rosé: Pink.

Rosso: Red (Italian).

Rouge: Red (French).

Schloss: Castle (German).

Sec: Dry.

Solera: Used for Sherry or Madeira. A process of drawing-off from old casks and re-filling from new.

Sommelier: Wine butler.

Spätlese: Late gathered grapes (German).

Spritzig: A slight amount of secondary fermentation giving to a still white wine a sense of life or prickle (German).

Spumante: Sparkling (Italian).

Table wine: Beverage wine.

Tawny: The reddy-brown colour of Port matured in the wood.

Tinto: Red (Spanish).

Trocken-Beeren-Auslese: Individually picked overripe grapes (German).

Vat: Tub. Traditionally made of oak, but frequently nowadays of glass-lined concrete.

Vendange: Grape harvest.

Vin: Wine (French).

Vin ordinaire: The most unpretentious of table wines.

Vino: Wine (Italian).

Weeper: A bottle with a defective cork.

Wein: Wine (German).

HOW TO UNDERSTAND A BRANDY LABEL

You will observe on Brandy bottles certain letters or stars. These indicate the approximate ages as follows:

1 *Star:* Equals two to three years' ageing in wood.

2 *Stars:* Equals three to four years' ageing in wood.

3 *Stars:* Equals minimum of five years' ageing in wood.

V.O. or *V.S.O.:* Equals five to ten years' ageing in wood.

V.S.O.P.: Minimum ten years' ageing in wood.

V.V.S.O.P.: Minimum twenty-five years' ageing in wood.

Some of you may wish to know what the above initials stand for so here is the answer:

V.O. means Very Old.

V.S.O. means Very Special Old.

V.S.O.P. means Very Special Old Pale.

V.V.S.O.P. means Very, Very Special Old Pale.

INDEX